Corporate Acquisitions and Mergers in Ukraine

Corporate Acquisitions and Mergers in Ukraine

Adam M. Mycyk

Dentons
Contributors

Oleksandra Piskun
Artur Savin
Tetiana Sokhotska
Valeria Tarasenko
Igor Svitlyk
Volodymyr Omelchenko

This book was originally published as a chapter in Corporate Acquisitions and Mergers.

General Editor: Peter Begg

Wolters Kluwer

Published by:
Kluwer Law International B.V.
PO Box 316
2400 AH Alphen aan den Rijn
The Netherlands
E-mail: international-sales@wolterskluwer.com
Website: lrus.wolterskluwer.com

Sold and distributed by:
Wolters Kluwer Legal & Regulatory U.S.
7201 McKinney Circle
Frederick, MD 21704
United States of America
E-mail: customer.service@wolterskluwer.com

ISBN 978-94-035-4011-5

e-Book: ISBN 978-94-035-4012-2
web-PDF: ISBN 978-94-035-4013-9

Contents

Dentons

Dentons is the world's first polycentric global law firm. Dentons' global team builds agile, tailored solutions to meet the local, national and global needs of private and public clients of any size in more than 205 locations serving 81 countries. Dentons' offices around the world provide the advantage of inter-connected collaboration for the benefit of its clients. Legal services in Ukraine are provided by LLC 'Dentons Europe'. Dentons has been active in Ukraine since 1988, and today Dentons' Kyiv office employs twenty-nine lawyers, including seven partners, dedicated full time to the Ukrainian practice. Dentons' Ukrainian practice encompasses the full range of legal services across a diverse range of industries. Dentons' international experience and in-depth knowledge of Ukrainian legislation, as well as its client-tailored approach, allow the team to provide clients with innovative, seamless legal solutions of the highest quality.

Author

Adam Mycyk is a partner in Dentons' Kyiv office. Adam has more than thirty years of experience advising both Ukrainian and international companies, banks, investment banks and a range of other financial institutions and investors on structuring and implementing debt and equity inward investments involving privatizations, mergers and acquisitions and joint ventures and on complex cross-border commercial and financing transactions and transaction on international capital markets. His experience and client base spans financial institutions and services, consumer products, retail, energy, manufacturing, telecommunications and agriculture sectors. Adam is a US qualified lawyer, admitted to the Bar in the District of Columbia (1993) and in Maryland (1991). Since relocating to Kyiv in 1994, he has led numerous acquisition and joint venture transactions and managed a variety of due diligence projects in various sectors.

1 INTRODUCTION

1.1 General Comments on the Country Profile

[01] Ukraine – a country in the geographical centre of Europe – is unique among the former Soviet Union republics, and one that, despite its often unfavourable notoriety in the press, remains a mystery for many. Since giving up the world's third-largest nuclear arsenal in 1994 (consisting of approx. 19 000 strategic nuclear warheads) in exchange for security assurances (but not guarantees, as we now know) provided by the United States, the United Kingdom and its largest neighbour to the east – Russia in the 1994 Budapest Memorandum, Ukraine by necessity learned to play a delicate balancing act between its western 'sponsor states', with their seemingly never-ending demands for difficult market and democratic reforms, and its more familiar eastern historical 'big brother'.

This balance was first upset in 2004 during the Orange Revolution, which brought Western-leaning President Victor Yushchenko to power, whose poisoning during his presidential campaign against Moscow-supported candidate Victor Yanukovych gave the world its first glimpse of how important Russia considers Ukraine to its sphere of influence. Yushchenko's tenure, to the dismay of many Ukrainians, did not bring about the anticipated swing of Ukraine firmly into the West's orbit, and this disenchantment led to the balance being temporarily restored in 2010 with Victor Yanukovych's successful presidential run.

President Yanukovych again attempted to play the East-West balancing act, but he seriously misjudged the deep European aspirations of the Ukrainian people when in November 2013 he abruptly pivoted on a long-negotiated Association Agreement with the European Union, foregoing that to focus instead on strengthening economic ties with Russia. This led to the now infamous Euromaidan protests (also known as the Revolution of Dignity), which eventually resulted in Yanukovych fleeing Ukraine to live in exile (in Russia – where else?).

The Ukrainian peoples' clear expression of a Euro-Atlantic course was not welcomed by Russia, which swiftly moved to annex part of Ukraine's territory – the Crimean peninsula –after a dubious referendum in early 2014. Soon thereafter, Russian-backed separatists began seizing territory in two of Ukraine's eastern regions – Luhansk and Donetsk – an ongoing conflict which has claimed over 13 000 Ukrainian lives, and which tragically resulted in the needless death of 298 people aboard Malaysian Airlines flight 17. Such brazen aggression from Ukraine's former 'brother nation' only served to cement the will of the majority of Ukrainians and their politicians towards a more European trajectory, which became evident when President Petro Poroshenko, elected after Yanukovych fled, finally signed the Association Agreement in May 2014, often described as Ukraine's 'first but most decisive step' towards EU membership.

Despite all of this upheaval and conflict, Ukraine – now helmed since 2019 by President Volodymyr Zelenskyy (an actor/comedian whose most famous role may now be in the First Impeachment Trial of President Donald J. Trump) – has, in recent years, continued to make tremendous strides in re-orienting itself towards the West, tipping the balance further away from its Eastern neighbour, Russia. But

Western support of course means Western demands – that unpalatable word 'reforms' again, and, frankly, some habits are hard to break. If one sits on one side of a see-saw for too long, when someone bigger sits on the other side it's often easier to ease up a little and start tipping the balance towards that side.

This time, however, another great power from the East – China – with its growing global influence seems ready to fill the vacant seat on the other side of the see-saw. The leadership of both countries have gradually been strengthening political and economic ties, having recently signed an agreement to promote Chinese infrastructure construction projects in Ukraine and announcing an intention to enter into a visa-free travel agreement between the two countries.

Ukraine may now find itself caught between China's Belt and Road initiative and the G7's recently announced 'Build Back Better World' (B3W) project, championed by US President Joe Biden's administration, which is aimed squarely at competing with the Belt and Road initiative. Some view this tilt as President Zelenskyy's response to the Biden administrations' recent lifting of sanctions against the Nord Stream 2 pipeline, which Ukraine views as a threat to its national security, and to President Biden's refusal of an urgent request to meet with President Zelenskyy before Biden's recent 'summit' with President Vladimir Putin of Russia. And you thought President Zelenskyy had a great phone call with former President Trump.

[02] You may be reading this now and thinking – why should we consider Ukraine? With its strategic geographic location, and its low production costs, Ukraine remains well-positioned to become a major service, manufacturing, supply chain and trading hub at the intersection of Europe and Asia. Once the most advanced scientific, industrial and agricultural republic of the former Soviet Union, Ukraine has maintained its leading position in terms of its intellectual potential whilst continuing to exploit its traditional export sectors, such as agriculture and natural resources, and becoming one of the top destinations for IT outsourcing. President Zelenskyy, in his introduction to the *UkraineInvest Guide: Explore Your Opportunities*, hails Ukraine as 'a new technological centre of the world, a breadbasket of Europe with the most fertile lands and a huge tourist and investment potential'. He urges people to 'Hurry up! The largest country in Europe is the next big thing.' As someone who, at this writing, has lived here for over twenty-seven years, I have to say that I think he's right!

[03] Ukraine is much larger than people unfamiliar with the country typically realize. Including Crimea (which Ukraine considers to be Ukrainian territory temporarily occupied by Russia, as evidenced by Ukraine's controversial football jersey at the recent Euro 2020 football championship featuring a map of Ukraine including the peninsula, much to the outrage of Russia), Ukraine has an area of 603 628 km2 (233 062 sq. mi), making it the largest country entirely within Europe, the second-largest country by area on the European continent, and the 46th largest country in the world. It borders Poland, Romania, Slovakia, Hungary and Moldova in the west (each of which, with the exception of Moldova, is already a member of the European Union (EU)), with Belarus and Russia to the north and the east, and via the Black Sea, Bulgaria, Georgia and Turkey to the south.

[04] Ukraine consists of twenty-four administrative regions – or 'oblasts' – and the Autonomous Republic of Crimea. The capital and largest city of Ukraine is Kyiv. Other major cities include Kharkiv, Dnipro (former Dnipropetrovsk), Donetsk, Odessa, Zaporizhzhya and L'viv.

[05] The country enjoys a range of natural resources (including iron ore, coal, oil, natural gas, shale gas and graphite) as well as many critical raw materials, such as lithium, cobalt, manganese and other rare earths, prompting the European Commission vice president Maroš Šefčovič to recently state that Ukraine could displace China as the EU's top 'supplier of raw materials and components for [carbon reducing] technologies of the future for Europe'. Historically, however, Ukraine is known as the 'breadbasket of Europe'. The vast size of its arable and farming areas, which cover 42 million sq.km (71% of the general area), is but one of the factors that accounts for this distinction. Ukraine's quality of black-coloured soil, known as chernozem, which contains a high percentage of humus, is among the largest in the world. And the market for that land has only recently been opened up, with the twenty-year moratorium on the sale of agricultural land having been lifted on 1 July 2021, as required to receive a loan from the International Monetary Fund (IMF). Ukrainian citizens will at first be able to purchase up to 100 hectares of land, and in 2024, the market will open up to agribusinesses who will be able to take part in auctions to acquire up to 10 000 hectares. Unfortunately, for the foreseeable future, the market will remain closed to foreign purchasers unless decided otherwise pursuant to a national referendum. Public opinion, however, is strongly against foreign ownership of Ukraine's most prized asset.

[06] Ukraine's southern borders rest on the Black Sea and the Sea of Azov, which, together with its large network of rivers, including the Dnipro, Danube, Dniester, Seversky Donets, Southern Bug, Pripyat and Desna, provides Ukraine with ample access to water transport (comprising of thirteen sea ports along mainland Ukraine). One of Ukraine's many challenges in managing its neighbour to the east is ensuring access to its ports, as the recent Russian naval build-up particularly in the Black Sea region and Russia's restriction of movement in the Azov Sea threaten Ukrainian shipping routes. A new Law on Concessions has already served as a backdrop for two new concession projects involving the Swiss-Georgian company Risoil, for a seaport concession in Kherson, and Qatari Q Terminal, which will be operating Olvia port in Mykolaiv. The tenders for these two pilot projects under the new law have been hailed as a testament to Ukraine's commitment to transparency and to encouraging foreign investment.

The country is also covered by an extensive road and rail transport network of close to 170 000 km of roadways, some 22 000 km of railways (excluding the temporarily occupied territory of the Autonomous Republic of Crimea, the city of Sevastopol), and over twenty passenger airports. Ukraine is continually improving its logistics infrastructure. According to the LPI index that ranks countries according to their logistic efficiency, Ukraine is at 66th place in the latest 2018 version of the index (out of 160 countries) in 2014. President Zelenskyy's Great Construction programme is an initiative to completely transform Ukraine's road transport infrastructure over the next three to four years. In 2021, the government has plans to repair 4 500 km of state and 2 000 km of local roads in 2021. The programme, however, is not just limited to roads, with projects underway to upgrade bridges, improve the rail network and the supply of locomotives and rolling stock, construction/reconstruction of regional airports, schools, hospitals, sports facilities and other ageing infrastructure, much of which was developed in the Soviet Union.

[07] Since independence, Ukraine's population has declined from a high of approximately 48 million people to approximately 41.50 million today, making it the 33rd most populous country in the world. The majority of Ukrainian citizens – 77.8% of the population – are ethnic Ukrainians, followed by a sizeable minority of Russians (17.3%) as well as Romanians/Moldovans, Belarusians, Crimean Tatars, and Hungarians.

[08] Ukrainian is the official language of Ukraine, and it uses the Cyrillic alphabet. A large portion of the population also speaks Russian, and the two languages are commonly used in business and socially. The dominant religion in the country is Eastern Orthodoxy, which has strongly influenced Ukrainian architecture, literature and music. In fact, Grand Prince Volodymyr the Great brought Christianity to the lands of Kyivan Rus in 988. When doing business with Ukraine, be advised that certain holidays commonly celebrated in other predominantly Christian parts of the world are celebrated in Ukraine according to the Orthodox (Julian) calendar, and not the Western (Gregorian) calendar (but note that since 2017 Christmas is now celebrated both on 7 January and on 25 December). It is thus advisable to consider the various local holidays when planning a business trip to Ukraine to ensure that your counterparties will actually be at work on those days!

[09] Ukraine has a very literate and highly educated population. The country is ranked the 4th most educated nation in the world, over 99.7% of Ukrainians are literate and over 70% have a secondary or higher education. Ukraine has over 2.5 million university students with some 640 000 graduates annually. Its IT sector is among its more prominent sectors, representing 8.3% of total exports in 2020, bringing it closer to the two largest export sectors – agriculture and metallurgy.

[10] As of January 2020, unemployment is reported to have averaged 9.2%, although unemployment in some regions, particularly in western Ukraine and central Ukraine, was significantly higher. During recent years unemployment continued fluctuating in the industrial eastern regions, and many large enterprises faced lay-offs due to severe economic challenges, including the loss of access to Russian and CIS markets. In addition, a number of industrial enterprises in the conflict zone were destroyed, robbed, dismantled and shipped to Russian territory. The COVID-19 pandemic hindered any improvement in the unemployment rate, with many service workers suffering as a result of various lockdowns.

[11] Recent statistics indicate that the average wage for the first four months of 2020 increased to 10 430 Ukrainian Hryvnia – approximately USD370, which is significantly below its regional peers. Low labour costs, coupled with its proximity to the large EU market, makes Ukraine a competitive alternative to Southeast Asia, especially for industries demanding short supply chains and fast production cycles.

In fact, the disruptions in global supply chains triggered by the COVID-19 pandemic have caused many companies to consider sourcing their supplies closer to their production facilities, making Ukraine an attractive location for companies supplying European manufacturers and looking for 'nearshoring' opportunities.

[12] The Ukrainian currency, Hryvnia (UAH), was launched by the National Bank of Ukraine (NBU) in 1996, shortly after the adoption of Ukraine's Constitution. In February 2014, the NBU abandoned the Hryvnia peg to the US Dollar, which until then had been set at a fixed rate (the last being UAH7.99 per USD1). Throughout its history, the UAH has gone through periods of rapid devaluation (generally occurring during periods of worldwide economic volatility) followed by longer periods of stability (primarily due to NBU interventions to maintain it at a fixed rate). As of this writing USD1 is worth roughly UAH27.30. The devaluation of the UAH has made Ukraine one of the most competitive low-cost production platforms globally. Labour, raw materials and other production costs have declined significantly in US dollar terms.

1.2 Government and Political System

[13] Ukraine is a unitary parliamentary-presidential republic, with state power divided among the legislative, executive and judicial branches of government. The general foundations of Ukraine's political system of Ukraine are contained in its Constitution.

Ukraine gained its independence in 1991, and its political and democratic institutions continue to evolve towards a more stable, democratic model. Over the years, the constant change of political direction and concentration of power in the hands of oligarch clans have resulted in two major periods of unrest since the beginning of this century alone. Changes in governments have also been frequent. As a result, the country and its political, economic and social systems have been in a relatively constant state of flux that for many years effectively hindered systematic and positive developments. In addition, the annexation of Crimea by Russia and the continuing unrest in certain parts of Eastern Ukraine plunged Ukrainian political, economic and social institutions into turmoil.

[14] As a result of the most recent popular unrest – EuroMaidan – at the end of 2013 and in early 2014, the then President Viktor Yanukovych fled the country. The unrest was precipitated by the Ukrainian government's decision not to sign a long-awaited and negotiated Association Agreement with the EU, but soon evolved into an outright protest against the President and his crony government, and the peaceful demonstrations eventually led to a government crackdown and significant bloodshed. On 21 March 2014, after Yanukovych fled, Ukraine signed the political portion of the Association Agreement with the EU.

[15] On 25 May 2014, Ukraine held presidential elections in which a clear majority of the population voted for Petro Poroshenko. President Poroshenko campaigned on a democratic platform designed to promote Ukraine's further integration into Europe. His election gave hope that Ukraine would finally proceed with fairly significant reforms that would contribute to a substantially improved business climate and long-term economic growth. After two decades of economic mismanagement, Ukrainians finally came to believe in a real chance to undergo a quantum leap in Ukraine's economic development. However, many Ukrainians sensed that the pace of reform under President Poroshenko had been too slow, and that the failure of the government to prosecute and punish many of those aligned with former President Yanukovych indicated that Ukraine was back to 'business as usual. This dissatisfaction manifested itself in a landslide victory in the 2019 presidential elections for current President Volodymyr Zelenskyy, who won with roughly 73% of the votes – a victory that many viewed as a punishment of Poroshenko by the electorate and not a reflection of the merits of President Zelenskyy's candidacy – a comedian, by profession, with no experience in government or politics.

[16] Immediately after his inauguration, President Zelenskyy dissolved Parliament, which resulted in snap elections being held in July 2019 (rather than in October, as scheduled). His Servant of the People party (named after the television show in which he starred as a teacher who unexpectedly wins the Ukrainian Presidential election) won 254 of the 450 seats in Parliament, providing the President with a one-party majority. Many would consider this to be a recipe for success, and whilst the Zelenskyy presidency backed by his party's parliamentary majority has had some notable successes, his first two years in office have been a mixed bag.

At the two-year mark, President Zelenskyy enjoys a much higher level of trust nationwide than his predecessors during the same period, with a 46% trust rating (compared to President Poroshenko, with a 20% trust rating, and President Yanukovych, with a 22% trust rating). Unlike his predecessors, the President has remained beyond suspicion when it comes to corruption. Despite the socio-economic situation remaining difficult for many Ukrainians, little progress being made in resolving the conflict in eastern Ukraine (a top priority for his presidency), and a less than stellar response in managing the COVID-19 pandemic (which led to the resignation of the Health Minister earlier in 2020), President Zelenskyy is viewed by many as the second-best president Ukraine has had in its thirty years of independence. Zelensky has demonstrated that he is not controlled by the oligarch, Igor Kolomoysky, his largest backer during his election campaign, and he and his parliamentary majority have managed to adopt several key laws, such as a new election law, the unbundling of Naftogaz, the lifting of the moratorium on the sale of agricultural land, a deregulation law (including the revoking of many regulations which had been in force since the USSR), the law increasing transparency of public finance, and the law regarding concessions which makes it easier for foreign companies to lease state-owned facilities.

[17] As a general observation, Ukraine is welcoming of foreign investors, although many areas of the economy tend to be dominated by local oligarchic groups that are generally averse to competition from foreign investors. Nonetheless, there are many success stories of foreign investors in Ukraine, and many well-known multinational and global companies either operate or are present on the market for many years.

In 2016, Ukraine created UkraineInvest as the government's investment promotion office, designed to attract foreign direct investment and assist existing investors to expand their businesses in Ukraine. UkraineInvest is committed 'to providing investors with "one-stop support" consisting of reliable, current information and advice on doing business in Ukraine; identifying optimal investment opportunities; guiding investors through government agencies at all levels; and helping to resolve any systemic issues investors may face'. Since its inception in 2016, UkraineInvest has unlocked USD3bn in foreign direct investment (including USD1.2bn in 2019), resolved 120+ legal and administrative issues of foreign investors, and provided 1 600+ consultations. UkraineInvest publish a very useful guide to investing in Ukraine, which can be accessed at their website: https://ukraineinvest.gov.ua/

Ukraine has also created a Business Ombudsman Council to help improve its investment climate. The Council, which is meant to be the first point of contact for companies seeking redress against unfair treatment, is financed from the Ukraine Stabilisation and Sustainable Growth Multi-Donor Account (MDA) managed by the European Bank for Reconstruction and Development (EBRD). The Council investigates complaints concerning alleged acts of corruption and other violations of legitimate interests of businesses by actions or omissions (including decisions) on the part of state and municipal authorities, businesses within the scope of their administration, and their officials. More information about the Council's activities and the types of cases they handle and assistance they provide can be found at their website: https://boi.org.ua/en/

In addition, the recent enactment of the so-called Investment Nanny law (discussed in more detail in the 'Incentives for Foreign Investment' section below), offers tax benefits and other forms of support to large investors in certain strategic areas of the economy and provides them with 'investment nannies', managers who will help them communicate with state officials, provide advice and generally help them navigate the complicated world that is Ukrainian bureaucracy. The law has been met with scepticism by some in the business community, who claim that a law alone will not cure systemic issues such as an unpredictable legal policy, corruption, and an ineffective judiciary. Only time will tell whether the government is able to effectively utilize the support mechanisms envisioned by the law to attract significant investment.

[18] Ukraine has been a member of the World Trade Organization (WTO) since 16 May 2008. Since 1 January 2016 the EU and Ukraine have provisionally applied their Deep and Comprehensive Free Trade Agreement (DCFTA). The creation of the DCFTA between Ukraine and the EU is set out in the economic section of EU-Ukraine Association Agreement, which was signed on 27 June 2014.

[19] Ukraine has concluded 17 free trade agreements with 47 countries, such as with the European Free Trade Association (EFTA), the CIS and also with Canada, the United Kingdom, Montenegro, Macedonia, Georgia, Azerbaijan, Uzbekistan, Tajikistan, Turkmenistan. For the time being, negotiation processes on the conclusion of bilateral Free Trade Agreements (FTAs) between Ukraine and Turkey, and the State of Israel are under way.

[20] The business climate continues to improve since President Zelenskyy and the new government and parliament took office. Notable key structural reforms in recent years include reforming the land market, relaunching privatization of state-owned enterprises, introducing a new Law on Concessions, enhancing the transparency of public procurement, simplifying business regulations, stabilizing and restructuring the banking sector, adopting the Law on Inland Water Transport and launching the Diia City Project aimed at creating favourable conditions for boosting Ukraine's IT sector.

[21] Significantly, in 2019 Ukraine rose in the World Bank's 'Doing Business' rankings to 64 out of 190 countries measured – a very welcome eight-place improvement since 2018.

1.3 Legal System

[22] The laws and regulations affecting Western investment and business in Ukraine continue to evolve, becoming more business and investor friendly. For historical reasons Ukraine lacks the extensive body of law, practice, precedent, certainty of application and effectiveness of enforcement normally encountered in Western business environments. The independence of the judiciary, and its insulation from economic, political and nationalistic influences is not entirely without doubt. Efforts to reform the judiciary have been piecemeal and slow, causing the IMF to suspend talks with Ukraine in February 2021 on a $700 million loan tranche due to the country's failure to deliver on several reforms, including overhauling the distrusted judiciary. At this writing, the Parliament just adopted in its second reading the last piece of legislation that will, at least in theory, allow reforming Ukraine's corrupt judiciary and put Ukraine back on track to receiving further IMF funds.

[23] In Ukraine, which has a civil law rather than a common law system, there does not exist a system of precedent. Courts will not necessarily enforce the laws as written or accessible and issue varying opinions, decisions and interpretations on the same law. In addition, courts in Ukraine lack experience in complex commercial dispute resolution, and many of the procedural remedies for enforcement and protection of legal rights typically found in Western jurisdictions are not available in Ukraine.

[24] Among the major problems of the Ukrainian judicial system are its incapacity and the lack of independence from prosecutorial influence. Ukraine is ranked 129 out of 105 countries with regard to judicial independence by the Global Competitiveness Index report 2019.

[25] Corruption remains one of Ukraine's biggest problems. Civil society is actively involved in combating and protesting against corruption and corporate raiding, although unfortunately there are still cases of criminal investigations against such activists. Compared to many of the former Soviet Union republics,

Ukrainian civil society is, however, very active and widespread, particularly after the EuroMaidan events.

[26] In short, Ukraine, like other former Soviet countries, suffers not only from a lack of suitable legislation and regulation and from considerable doubt as to how the courts will interpret the existing laws and rules, but from the concomitant absence of a belief in and respect for the rule of law. One Canadian political commentator, Yuri Polakiwsky, recently commented in one of his articles on a proposed law designed to reign in the influence of Ukrainian oligarchs that 'to understand Ukraine is to comprehend that it remains a society in which there is no societal commitment to the underlying value of the rule of law and "good" behavior'. Perhaps a harsh criticism, but one that should make every Ukrainian consider what they do in their everyday lives that perpetuate this societal problem.

[27] Notwithstanding this, reforms continue, particularly on the anti-corruption front, and the various deficiencies noted above are – in some form or another – being tackled, at least on paper. This is a key area of reform, and one that is being very closely monitored not only by Ukraine's foreign donors but also by Ukraine's business community. A recent survey conducted by the American Chamber of Commerce in Ukraine, entitled Ukraine Business Climate Survey: A Year of Lockdown, noted the following three biggest obstacles cited by members (consisting of a mix of foreign and Ukrainian companies) to doing business in Ukraine: the lack of rule of law (66%), corruption (54%), and the lack of a bold reform agenda (45%). Members also pointed to the top three things that Ukraine's Government should focus on to achieve economic recovery and growth in 2021: implement real and effective judicial reform, rule of law, fair justice (74%), protect the population from COVID-19 through wide-scale testing, vaccination, and effective treatment (46%), and eradicate corruption (37%). Reform . . . there goes that ugly word again.

1.4 Current Economic Aspects

[28] Since its independence in 1991 Ukraine has attracted a notable amount of foreign investment, although relatively much less than neighbouring countries in the region. During the last thirty years, levels of M&A activity have been mixed due to a combination of various local and external factors. One of the major local factors that negatively impacted M&A activity was the absence of a clear course for economic development. The absence of political stability, poorly designed reform and development policies, inadequate legislation, absence of the rule of law, monopolism of the economy, discriminatory taxation and high levels of corruption at virtually all levels of government led to a slow and difficult transition from a Soviet planned economy to a market-based economy.

[29] Since the EuroMaidan movement the Ukrainian government has faced acute political, security, and economic challenges. Moreover, the recent economic downturn resulting from the COVID-19 pandemic, as well as the ongoing military conflict and continuing Russian aggression, have not done much to foster interest from foreign investors, many of whom fail to appreciate the highly localized nature of the current military conflict.

[30] Key reforms have been undertaken by the government since 2014, including: carrying out significant fiscal consolidation, moving to a flexible exchange rate, reforming energy tariffs and social assistance, enhancing the transparency of public procurement, simplifying business regulations, stabilizing and restructuring the banking sector, moving forward on health and pension reforms, and establishing anti-corruption agencies. Although recent statistics indicate some economic turnaround, the last few years have been difficult. Ukraine's industrial production fell by over 0.5% in 2019 compared to 2018 and decreased a further 5.2% in 2020. Gross Domestic Product (GDP) grew by 3.3% in 2018, by 3.2% in 2019, but decreased by 4.4% in 2020. Projections for GDP growth in 2021 are roughly 4%, which effectively represents a rebound that will cancel out 2020's GDP decline. Second quarter 2021 statistics released by the Economy Ministry in July indicate that Ukraine's GDP grew by 6% year-on-year in the second quarter, coming after five straight quarters of decline due to the coronavirus pandemic.

[31] In terms of the national currency, the Ukrainian hryvnia (or UAH), in 2014, the National Bank of Ukraine adopted a fluctuating/floating currency in an attempt to meet IMF requirements and to try to enforce a stable foreign exchange market. As a result, the UAH lost approximately 70% of its value against the US dollar, but it has managed to remain under UAH30 to USD1 since then. The Ministry of Economic Development predicts that the dollar will rise in price by 2024 but will not cross the UAH30 mark, with a 2021 exchange rate of UAH29.1/USD, increasing slightly in 2022 to UAH29.3/USD, and further in 2023 to UAH29.5/USD.

Economists note that one of the key reasons for Ukraine's relatively good economic performance in 2020 was the country's macroeconomic development. International currency reserves increased to USD29.1bn by the end of 2022, compared to USD25.3bn at the end of 2019, representing the highest level since 2011. Foreign trade in 2020 stimulated this increase, because prices for primary exports such as agricultural goods, iron ore, and steel all rose, while the price of energy imports fell, resulting in a current account surplus equal to 4% of GDP.

[32] Foreign direct investment to Ukraine in 2019 grew to USD51.4bn, representing an increase over 2018 statistics of USD44bn. Statistics for the first nine months of 2021 indicated foreign direct investment of USD49bn, largely concentrated in the following sectors: manufacturing, trade, mining and quarrying, financial and insurance, real estate, utilities, and IT and communications. The National Bank of Ukraine recently noted that foreign direct investment in the first quarter of 2021 amounted to USD1 486m.

[33] Ukraine has, however, become a large recipient of foreign aid and assistance. Notably, the IMF was quick to begin its support of Ukraine when, in April 2014, it approved a USD17.5bn four-year extended fund facility programme for Ukraine. In June 2020, the IMF approved a USD5bn stand-by loan with an immediate payment of USD2.1bn to help fight the COVID-19 pandemic. Four other tranches that were scheduled in 2020 and in 2021 have not been disbursed due to the slow pace of reforms. The Ukrainian government still hopes to receive a tranche of about USD0.7bn in 2021, which experts say is crucial before September 2021 when Ukraine is due to make USD40m in external debt payments. Ukraine has been taking crucial steps towards meeting IMF demands for the release of these payments, particularly, as noted above, in the area of judicial reform. The IMF has welcomed the recent approval of the judicial reform bills but expects more progress in other sectors before releasing funds. Receiving an IMF tranche yet in 2021 would trigger the release of EUR600m from the EU and USD350m from the World Bank.

The US, Canada, the EU, as well as a number of international financial institutions and development banks, continue to provide a large amount of financial and technical assistance to Ukraine and its institutions. Since 2014 US assistance to Ukraine totals over USD3.7 billion, plus three USD1 billion sovereign loan guarantees. Such assistance has in recent years also included military assistance, with the Pentagon announcing in March 2021 a USD125m military aid package for Ukraine, the first of its kind under the Biden administration.

[34] To help increase revenues, Ukraine has forecast more than USD430m in budget revenues from privatization in 2021, with USD320m expected to come via large-scale privatization, and the remaining USD110m from the sale of smaller objects.

[35] The State Property Fund, which oversees privatizations, is, under its current head Dmytro Sennychenko, actively seeking to sell the over 3 500 state-owned enterprises remaining in government ownership and is concentrating on creating transparent conditions for the upcoming privatization auctions and expanding the participant list as much as possible. Privatization rules generally apply to both foreign and domestic investors, and, in theory, a relatively level playing field exists. Historically, past privatizations have not been entirely transparent, and, as is the case in many countries of the former Soviet Union, many were criticized as having been adjusted to fit a pre-selected bidder.

State-owned companies offered for privatization can be bought by any Ukrainian or foreign individual or company, with certain exceptions, including among others: companies registered in offshore zones with non-transparent ownership structures; citizens, residents and companies originating from an aggressor state (e.g., Russia), and companies in which an aggressor state holds an equity interest or is controlled by an aggressor state; companies whose beneficial owner of 10% or more shares is a resident of an aggressor state, with the exception of companies whose shares are traded on a stock exchange (from the list approved by the Government of Ukraine); companies registered in states included on the Financial Action Task Force (FATF) blacklist, as well as affiliates of such companies; and individuals and companies under sanctions and their affiliates.

[36] The government's plans for large scale privatization were, unfortunately, put on hold in 2020 as a result of the COVID-19 pandemic. On 29 April 2021, a law removing the temporary hold on large-scale privatization was signed by President Zelenskyy. The Head of the State Property Fund soon announced a list of companies that will be the first to be offered for sale in 2021: United Mining and Chemical Company (a top producer of titanium ore concentrates), which is expected to generate considerable interest; First Kyiv Machine-Building Plant; and the President-Hotel (a four-star hotel in Kyiv city centre). Other companies slated for privatization in 2021 include Odesa Portside Plant (producer of mineral fertilizers), Coal Company 'Krasnolymanska' (coal mining and extraction) and Elektrovazhmash (producer of power generators), as well as a number of state-owned power generation and power distribution companies. The State Property Fund has engaged the services of international and local investment advisers to assist with the sales.

[37] As the countries around the world adjusted to life during the COVID-19 pandemic in 2020 and attempted to manage the negative economic effects of the crisis, Ukraine was no exception. Although estimates were for GDP to grow by 3.5% in 2020, the National Bank of Ukraine noted that in 2020, Ukrainian GDP fell by 4.4%. Although Ukraine had been witnessing year-on-year growth in M&A activity in the years since the EuroMaidan protests, 2020 witnessed a significant decline of just over 60% from 2019 to just over USD900 000 (based on disclosed transactions). Deal volume fell by 15% from 2019 to approximately 69 transactions, with average transaction values of approximately USD28m.

Much of the M&A transactions in 2020 were domestic transactions, which represented roughly 62% of all deals and approximately 55% of the overall transaction volumes. The majority of these transactions – just over half – were focused in the following sectors: real estate and construction, agriculture, the IT sector, and oil and gas, which represented nearly 90% of the overall domestic transaction volumes.

During this same period, foreign investors' M&A activity tended to focus on three main sectors: technology, agriculture and transport and infrastructure, with one-third of the 25 announced deals having been undertaken by new market entrants. These investors primarily came from three key regions: Europe, the Middle East, and North America, with deals undertaken by these investors representing roughly 83% of the overall inbound M&A value and approximately 92% of transaction volume. Overall inbound M&A represented nearly one-third of overall deal volume.

[38] Other notable sectors for M&A activity in 2020 included consumer markets, oil and gas, metals and mining, banking and insurance, and healthcare and pharmaceuticals.

[39] The most attractive sectors in the foreseeable future will continue to be agriculture, IT, real estate and construction, and transportation and infrastructure. EU and European investors are expected to continue investing in Ukraine's renewable energy sector, and in particular in wind and solar, although further investment into this sector will be closely watched to see how the government manages its significant debt obligations to current producers. Notable interest may be seen in Ukraine's potential for green hydrogen production, with Ukraine having been named as a partner in the European Hydrogen Strategy, there being an intention to utilize Ukraine's gas transportation system to transport green hydrogen to the EU. In late June 2021, German Ambassador to Ukraine Anka Feldhusen urged Ukraine to begin preparing its gas transmission system for the transit of hydrogen, noting Germany's commitment to shifting its industry entirely to hydrogen over fifteen years. Further signalling Ukraine as an attractive destination for investment, in February 2021 Ukraine and the United Arab Emirates signed a number of memoranda and contracts totalling USD3bn.

[40] All of these factors combined, however, mean that many good Ukrainian assets are quite undervalued, and there are a myriad of promising opportunities for an astute foreign investor seeking long-term growth in a highly promising European market. As the situation in Ukraine improves, with more aid from foreign donors helping to fill in budgetary gaps and provide technical assistance for the ongoing monumental reform process, asset prices are bound to reach pre-pandemic levels within the next few years.

[41] Nevertheless, Ukraine remains a high-risk country. The country is, essentially, in a very localized war in parts of the Donetsk and Luhansk oblasts, and this, coupled with the annexation of Crimea, has led to the devastation of an important industrial region, along with the industrial and social infrastructure therein. The conflict resulted in disruption of business in the conflict zone and a deterioration of relations with Russia, and these negative effects coupled with the COVID-19 pandemic's negative impact on Ukraine's GDP and the concomitant slowdown of the privatization programme, have led to a significant reduction of foreign direct investment.

1.5 Main Industries

[42] Ukraine's principal economic sectors include agriculture, metallurgy, industry, mining, oil and gas transit, fuel and energy, electricity generation, nuclear power, construction and IT.

[43] Ukraine is the world's third-largest grain producer (behind the United States and the EU) and has generally been a profitable country for foreign investors. Domestically oriented sectors like the consumer and retail sectors have traditionally attracted foreign direct investment more than export-oriented manufacturing. Within the manufacturing sector, metallurgy and food processing have attracted investors ahead of machine building and the chemical industry.

[44] Ukraine deserves special mention regarding its IT service and software R&D sector – this sector has demonstrated double-digit growth year-over-year. The export volume of Ukraine's software development industry grew by 20.4% in 2020 (pushing the sector above USD5bn for the first time) and is considered the number-three export sector (representing 8.3% of all exports, after agriculture and metallurgy). This sector of Ukraine's economy shows great potential due to the country's large, skilled workforce. Ukraine's approximately 200 000 IT specialists are primarily concentrated in certain key industry hubs in Kyiv, Lviv, Kharkiv, Odesa, and Dnipro. Well-known Ukrainian product companies such as Grammarly,

Preply or People.ai all originate from Ukraine, indicating that the market is evolving from its long history of outsourcing companies to product companies with global reach.

A new law, adopted on 15 July 2021, is intended to create the most powerful IT hub in Central and Eastern Europe in Ukraine. The Law 'On Stimulation of the Development of the Digital Economy in Ukraine' ('Diia City Law'), which currently awaits President Zelenskyy's signature, introduces a general framework for launching a special IT industry regime called Diia City.

Ukrainian companies that meet the following criteria will be able to take advantage of the benefits provided by the Diia City Law, in particular:

- minimum average monthly remuneration of employees/gig workers of EUR1 200;
- engaged in IT-related activities, which include, among others, software development activities, games publishing, and data processing, cybersport;
- at least nine employees or gig workers at the end of each calendar month; and
- net income from qualified activities is at least 90% of total income.

Diia City Law introduces a number of concepts designed to harmonize the business rules for qualifying 'Diia City residents' to those commonly found in other countries by introducing, among others:

- gig contracts;
- social guarantees for gig workers;
- requirements for non-disclosure and non-compete agreements;
- convertibility of outstanding debt into equity of Diia City residents;
- warranty concepts and compensation for misrepresentation;
- additional regulation for put/call option agreements;
- the ability to subject shareholders agreements to foreign law.

Parliament also plans to adopt a new law 'On Amendments to the Tax Code of Ukraine regarding the Stimulation of the Development of Digital Economy in Ukraine' No. 5376 to govern the tax regime applicable to Diia City residents and their workers. This draft law currently contemplates that Diia City residents may choose one of two tax regimes: either the currently existing corporate income tax (CIT) at a standard rate of 18%, or a new regime providing for CIT at a rate of 9% on volumes of certain transactions with non-payers of CIT. Benefits for employees/gig workers engaged by Diia City residents contemplated by the draft law include, among others, a reduced personal income tax on salary/remuneration at a rate of 5% (as opposed to the general 18% rate).

More information about Diia City can be found at its website: https://city.diia.gov.ua/en.

[45] In addition, Ukraine's energy sector is particularly ripe for investment, given Ukraine's policy of becoming more independent in respect of its own energy needs. The country's renewable energy sector had been attracting a fair amount of investor interest, given Ukraine's favourable 'green tariff' for producers of energy from renewable sources. During the Yanukovych years, Ukraine introduced attractive high green tariff rates to attract investment in wind and solar energy production, which indeed led to significant investment in the sector by foreigners and domestic investors. In 2020, however, the government amassed significant arrears to producers of about USD1bn. Coupled with recent retroactive cuts to the tariffs to levels that the government believes are more sustainable, the government's treatment of these arrears has deterred foreigners from investing in Ukraine altogether and has hampered the investment plans of many renewables investors. Reports indicate that as of this writing, renewable energy producers are pursuing 130 legal actions totalling USD66m against the government's 'guaranteed buyer' of renewable energy for non-payment of the green tariff. The government is apparently considering placing a 'green bond' to pay off the overdue debt of roughly USD630m.

Notwithstanding the problems faced in the industry, given the potentially large green hydrogen market in Europe, Ukraine has the potential to utilize its renewable energy sector to become one of Europe's major green hydrogen suppliers. The risk that Nord Stream 2 poses to Ukraine's transit pipeline infrastructure (including the potential loss of up to USD3bn in annual transit fees) can be mitigated by refocusing the pipelines to deliver green hydrogen to Europe.

As noted above, Ukraine possesses many critical raw materials such as lithium, cobalt, manganese and other rare earths, and these deposits are garnering interest from the EU, which one EU official recently noting that EU mining and metals processing investments in Ukraine could win insurance cover from the new European Fund for Sustainable Development. Ukraine's Prime Minister, Denys Shmyhal, notes that long-term investment in Ukraine's mining sector could generate $400 billion over the next decade, and that Ukraine should aim to be a full partner of the EU in the extraction and processing of critical raw materials, rather than a 'raw material donor'. The EU's recognition of Ukraine's potential in this sector was recently confirmed by the signing of a Memorandum on Strategic Partnership in the Raw Materials Sector and a corresponding Roadmap between the EU and Ukraine.

Notably, labour is Ukraine's second-largest export, after food, and ahead of metals, which results in a large influx of foreign currency remittances to Ukraine. Many EU countries – facing labour shortages – compete for Ukrainian workers. The National Bank of Ukraine predicts that in 2021, remittances from Ukrainians working abroad – largely in the EU – is expected to increase by 8% to USD13bn.

[46] Foreign investors in Ukraine have over the years consisted of not only strategic investors but also a fair mix of private equity and venture capital and other financial investors. Given the relatively distressed state of the economy, we would expect to see more interest from funds focused on distressed assets in the near term, with strategic investors and more traditional private equity buyers in the region returning to the market as soon as the first signs of economic stabilization become more evident.

1.6 Cultural Aspects

[47] 'Ukraine is open and ready for business.' This phrase is quite often repeated by various high-level Ukrainian officials in an attempt to cultivate interest in Ukraine's economy. Current market conditions create real opportunities for both new entrants to the Ukrainian market as well as foreign investors already operating in Ukraine.

[48] Aside from ownership of agricultural land, the regulatory framework for the establishment and operation of business in Ukraine by foreign investors is generally similar to that for domestic investors. Foreign and domestic private entities can establish and own business enterprises and engage in all forms of commercial activity. Investment permits are not required, but all enterprises must be established according to the form and procedure prescribed by law and registered with the appropriate state authorities. Foreign companies are restricted from owning agricultural land, manufacturing carrier rockets, and some publishing activities. In addition, Ukrainian law authorizes the government to set limits on foreign participation in 'strategically important areas', but the wording is vague, and the law is rarely used in practice. Generally, these restrictions limit the maximum permissible percentage of foreign investment into Ukrainian firms in these sectors.

[49] Business activities in Ukraine are often subject to licensing by different state agencies. Moreover, starting up a business usually means registering with the tax and pension authorities, among others, and obtaining numerous permits and approvals, such as fire safety, labour, sanitary, and others. Since 2006, the state has been working to set up a network of 'one-stop-shops' where entrepreneurs can register with all necessary entities in a single location and cut down the amount of time required to set up shop. Efforts at simplification continue.

[50] Although the ease of doing business has greatly improved over the nearly thirty years of Ukraine's independence, businesses nonetheless occasionally feel the strains from Ukraine's long history of heavy bureaucratic interference and burdens and strict government regulation. Nevertheless, before starting a project in Ukraine, an investor should obtain qualified local advice because Ukrainian laws tend to be vague, allowing for different interpretations. Ukraine is, after all, still considered a high-risk country, particularly given the ongoing tensions with Russia. Risk mitigation ultimately depends on the facts and circumstances of the proposed business venture, and qualified local advisors can assist in assessing those risks and suggesting steps for mitigation. Generally, as is the case in other countries, the less regulated a particular line of business is, the easier it is to operate. The best defence to any problem is to always ensure that your house is in order and to be prepared to defend your position if challenged. For example, although the tax authorities have historically been known to be quite aggressive, practice shows that, on average, tax disputes are resolved in favour of the taxpayer.

[51] As a general matter, Ukraine is not a particularly expensive place to do business. Kyiv, the capital, is the most expensive city in the country, with hotel accommodations and expatriate living expenses rivalling those of most major world capitals. Other areas of Ukraine are, however, quite moderate when compared to the capital. Advisors range from some of the world's top law, accounting, consulting and other professional advisory firms to smaller independent Ukrainian firms, and their fees range accordingly, depending on the level and scope of advice. Often Western businesspeople find the cost of professional services to be more expensive than they anticipated, and smaller, less experienced investors may find doing business in Ukraine much more expensive than in other developed countries.

[52] In terms of the cultural peculiarities of doing business in Ukraine, we note a few of the more common ones below:

1.6.1 Hospitality

[53] Ukrainians are known for their generous hospitality. You may often find yourself being invited as a guest to someone's home after a particularly successful business meeting, in which case you should be prepared to bring along your appetite together with a small gift of flowers or wine. Important delegations are often given the 'red carpet' treatment, and occasionally the hospitality precedes the actual conduct of business. The closing of a transaction is usually quite a celebrated affair, and toasts are a normal part of any such celebration! Be prepared for many toasts – and remember to bring along your aspirin for the morning after!

1.6.2 Language

[54] Although English is quite prevalent in business (and in various governmental bodies), key decision makers often do not speak any language other than Ukrainian and/or Russian. Government officials tend to have interpreters at high-level meetings, and larger businesses often engage English-speaking investment bankers or other professionals to advise them on transactions. It is, however, advisable for the non-Ukrainian or non-Russian speaker to be accompanied by a qualified interpreter or other bi-lingual advisor to help ensure that nothing gets lost in translation. In terms of everyday services, English is quite common among younger adults, and personnel at hotels and restaurants typically have a good command of English; taxi drivers unfortunately do not.

1.6.3 Punctuality and Reliability in Ukraine

[55] Being late for meetings is quite common in Ukraine. Generally, the more important your counterpart is – whether a private businessman or a government official – the later he or she will be. In addition, meetings with government officials are frequently rescheduled and cancelled, often at the last minute. It's generally advisable to confirm meetings close to the scheduled time. Bear in mind that traffic in Kyiv during business hours can be quite heavy (Kyiv ranks 7th in the TomTom Traffic Index), and travel time should be planned accordingly.

1.6.4 Never Underestimate the Power of Bureaucracy

[56] When dealing with the government, whether directly on a project or as part of a larger project in which a government approval or consent is required, it is generally best to factor in slightly more time than what the law – or the relevant government officials – may tell you is needed. Despite the removal of many obstacles to doing business, Ukraine is still a very formalistic and bureaucratic society, and if a stamp is missing or a translation was not properly notarized or a document not legalized/apostilled, you may face considerable delays. The offices of many governmental and administrative bodies are often quite hectic and disorganized, with long lines. You may often find yourself being asked to produce documents or carry out other formalities that are not in line with publicly available rules. A token gift, such as a box of chocolates or a bottle of cognac, often tend to smooth over any misunderstandings with lower-level functionaries. Also note that very often, entrance into official buildings, and even private office buildings, requires that some form of identification be produced, so do not lock away your passport in the hotel safe!

1.6.5 How Important Are Personal Connections in Ukraine?

[57] Ukrainians tend to prize the power of personal contacts, particularly contacts in government, as relations between government and business have generally been less than collaborative. In addition, although Ukrainians prefer to hold business meetings in person, the COVID-19 pandemic has forced Ukrainians – much as the rest of the world – to embrace the benefits (and pitfalls) of video-conferencing services.

1.6.6 Leadership Styles in Ukraine

[58] Leadership styles in Ukrainian organizations often differ from what most Westerners are used to, and Westerners may be frustrated by what often appears to be a reluctance to take on responsibility for a decision, particularly within governmental institutions. Leaders (both in government and in the private sector) often display an authoritarian attitude towards their subordinates, and Westerners may find this somewhat off-putting at first. Delegation is generally not the rule, particularly with high-level decisions, which leaders tend to keep within their own control. Although women are generally becoming more visible at the top echelons of government and business, Ukraine is still a relatively male-dominated society and quite socially conservative.

2 REGULATORY FRAMEWORK

2.1 Business Vehicles

[59] Ukrainian legislation envisages a number of corporate forms which a legal entity may take in Ukraine. These comprise:

- Joint Stock Company (JSC);
- Limited Liability Company (LLC);
- additional liability company;
- general partnership; and
- limited partnership.

[60] JSCs and LLCs are the corporate forms most commonly used, and foreign investors prefer their subsidiaries or joint ventures to be organized in either of these two forms. Such preference is likely to be based on the fact that the applicable legislation states that participants in LLCs and shareholders of JSCs are personally liable only to the extent of their participation interest/shareholding in the declared (charter) capital in these types of legal entities, whereas participants of additional liability companies and general partnerships (but not limited partnerships) are individually liable for the obligations of such companies/partnerships. This section focuses on JSCs and LLCs as the most common forms.

[61] Foreign citizens, foreign entities, individuals without citizenship and international organizations may all act as founders of JSCs and LLCs, on the same basis as Ukrainian citizens and legal entities.

[62] Foreign companies may also set up representative offices and branches in Ukraine, but they do not qualify as separate legal entities under Ukrainian law.

[63] As between an LLC and a JSC, an LLC is the more commonly used form, given its relative simplicity, in terms of both registration/establishment and corporate governance/operation. Generally speaking, the procedure for the incorporation and the operation of an LLC is significantly less burdensome and time-consuming, because LLCs do not issue shares and are not required to make public disclosures of corporate information or to carry out other reporting, as with JSCs.

2.2 Joint Stock Company

[64] A JSC is a company in which the charter capital is divided into a specific number of shares of equal par value, similar to US corporations and UK limited companies. Activities of JSCs are regulated principally by the Civil Code of Ukraine, dated 16 January 2003 (Civil Code), the Commercial Code of Ukraine, dated 16 January 2003 (Commercial Code), the Law on Joint Stock Companies, dated 17 September 2008 (JSC Law), the Law on Securities and Stock Market dated 23 February 2006 (Securities and Stock Market Law).

[65] Under the JSC Law, JSCs are classified into public JSCs and private JSCs. Public JSCs may place their shares both publicly and privately, whereas private JSCs may only privately place their shares. Shares issued by a public JSC must be listed on a stock market. Public JSCs must also be audited in accordance with International Financial Reporting Standards (IFRS). Under the JSC Law, shares may exist only in electronic form.

[66] A JSC may be established and may be owned by a single shareholder (either a legal entity or an individual). However, JSCs may not be established by a legal

entity which itself has only one participant. The personal liability of shareholders is limited to the value of shares owned.

[67] To establish a JSC, the company must have a minimum charter capital of 1 250 times the Ukrainian official minimum monthly salary as of the day of its formation (the current minimum monthly salary is UAH6 000 and the minimum capital requirement is therefore UAH7 500 000, which is the equivalent of approx. USD277 800). Any issuance of shares by private and public JSCs must be registered by the National Commission on Securities and Stock Market (Securities Commission) and a corresponding certificate must be issued.

[68] Shares of a public JSC are freely tradable on stock exchanges, with no requirement for a shareholder to obtain prior consent of other shareholders or the company before transferring shares. In contrast, shares of a private JSC are distributed among co-founders and may not be publicly traded. A pre-emptive right of shareholders of a private JSC to purchase shares offered by other shareholders may be envisaged by the charter of the relevant private JSC but is not required by law. If such right is envisaged by the charter, the procedure for its exercise must be followed as set out in the JSC Law.

[69] Under the general rule, in the event of a change of control in a JSC (when one or more affiliated entities acquire 50% or more of the shares), the purchaser(s) must offer to buy out the shares of the remaining shareholders.

[70] JSCs are obliged to make public disclosure of their financial statements and other information (e.g., change of management, shareholders) on an annual, quarterly and ad hoc basis.

[71] The procedure of incorporation of a new JSC is more time-consuming, as compared to an LLC, and may take up to two to three months.

2.3 Corporate Governance in JSCs

[72] The corporate governance structure of a JSC consists of a (i) General Shareholders' Meeting (GSM), (ii) a Supervisory Board, (iii) a Management Board and (iv) an Audit Committee.

2.3.1 GSM

[73] The GSM is the highest governing body of a JSC and determines the policy of the company. All shareholders, regardless of the quantity and type of shares owned, are entitled to participate in a GSM. Members of other bodies of the JSC may also participate in a GSM, though without any voting rights. Shareholders have a right to vote on the principle of one-share-one-vote, except when a cumulative voting mechanism applies.

[74] A valid GSM is constituted when more than 50% of the shares eligible to vote are in attendance. Shareholders have the right to appoint a proxy to attend the

GSM and vote on their behalf. According to the JSC Law, shareholder meetings have exclusive competence to decide, *inter alia*, the following matters:

- defining the main objectives of the company's activity;
- making amendments to the charter;
- change of the company's type (private or public);
- cancellation of the redeemed shares;
- emission of the company's shares;
- emission of securities that can be converted into shares;
- splitting or consolidation of the company's shares;
- increasing/ decreasing the charter capital;
- approval and amendment of internal regulations on the GSM, Supervisory Board, Audit Committee, Management Board;
- approval of the amount of annual dividends;
- approval of regulations on remuneration of members of the Supervisory Board;
- approval of the report on remuneration of members of the Supervisory Board;
- approval of an annual report;
- approval of reports of the Supervisory Board, the Management Board, the Audit Committee;
- consideration of findings of the external audit and approval of measures based on the results of its consideration;
- distribution of profit and losses;
- decisions on issues regarding the procedure for holding the GPM;
- election/termination of members of the Supervisory Board, approval of terms and conditions of civil law agreements, labour agreements (contracts) to be executed with such members, determination of their remuneration, election of a person to be authorized to sign agreements (contracts) with the members of the Supervisory Board;
- election/termination of the Audit Committee (Auditor);
- election/termination of members of the counting commission;
- approval of a material transaction;
- termination/liquidation of the company, appointment of a liquidation commission, approval of the procedure and period of liquidation, etc.

[75] The JSC charter may include other issues to be decided by the GSM. Typically, such additional items include the approval of certain significant corporate contracts, appointment of executive officers, creation of corporate internal rules and other similar issues.

2.3.2 Supervisory Board

[76] The Supervisory Board controls the activities of a JSC's executive body, the Management Board, and should protect the rights of the company's shareholders. A JSC with over ten shareholders is required by law to establish a Supervisory Board. The members of the Supervisory Board may only be elected from among the individuals being the JSC shareholders, their representatives and/or independent directors. The members of the Supervisory Board may not also be members of the same JSC's Management Board or Audit Committee.

[77] A public JSC and any JSC in which 50% or more of all shares are state owned, are be required to have no less than two non-executive members on its Supervisory Board (the so-called independent directors). An independent director shall meet the independence criteria set forth by the JSC Law. In a public JSC the number of Supervisory Board members must be five or more. The Supervisory Board members of a public JSC shall be elected through cumulative (i.e., proportional) voting (i.e., for a resolution to appoint Supervisory Board members a shareholder will have one vote per each share held, multiplied by the number of Supervisory Board members to be elected).

[78] The JSC Law also contains a concept of an 'interested party' transaction, pursuant to which certain transactions involving an 'interested party' require approval of the Supervisory Board or GSM. A party is deemed 'interested' under the JSC Law if it is (i) a shareholder holding 25% or more of the JSC's shares, (ii) a company official or certain of his/her relatives or (iii) an affiliate. An interested party should inform the Management Board, which in turn should inform the Supervisory Board, of its interest in the transaction. A failure by an interested party to observe its duty to inform could lead to it being held liable for any damage caused to the company as a result of the transaction and a court ruling the transaction invalid.

2.3.3 Management Board

[79] The Management Board is the executive body of a JSC that manages day-to-day operations of the company. It can be a collective (board of directors, directorate) or sole (director, general director) authority. The general director normally acts on behalf of the company without a power of attorney. The charter of a JSC should stipulate whether the members of the Management Board are elected by the GSM or the Supervisory Board.

[80] The Management Board reports to the GSM and the Supervisory Board and is obliged to organize the implementation of their decisions. It acts on behalf of a JSC within the limits established by its charter and the law.

[81] The Civil Code and the JSC Law impose a duty on officers of the Management Board (and the company's other governing bodies) to act in good faith in the company's interests within the scope of their powers.

2.3.4 Audit Committee

[82] The Audit Committee carries out audit control over the financial and business activities of a JSC's Management Board. Members of the Management Board or the Supervisory Board cannot be members of the Audit Committee. The Audit Committee's authority derives from statute, and (at least in theory) it has fairly broad authority to control the financial activity of the company, to review company documents, participate in management meetings and audit the activities of the company's bodies.

[83] The Audit Committee also has an investigatory role, in so far as it is obliged to conduct investigations (e.g., in case of violations or inaction by the Company's managers) and inspections following a request from either the holders of more than 10% of the company's shares, the GSM, the Supervisory Board or on its own initiative in cases stipulated by the JSC's charter.

[84] In order for the GSM to approve the company's annual balance sheet, the Audit Committee is required to prepare an annual report on the activities of the company.

2.4 Limited Liability Company

[85] The ownership interest of investors (referred to as 'participants') in an LLC is expressed by 'participation interests' in the capital of the company, rather than by shares or stock. An LLC's capital is set out in its charter, and each participant owns a percentage of the capital. The personal liability of a participant of an LLC is limited to the value of the participant's respective contribution to the company's capital. An LLC may be founded by one or more participants.

[86] To establish an LLC, the founder(s) must file the following documents with the Ukrainian registration authority: resolution to establish an LLC, proof of the founder's identity, a charter (articles of association) of the LLC, documents confirming the identity of the ultimate beneficial owners of the LLC (if available), a corporate structure chart up until the ultimate beneficial owners and a standard registration form. After registration with the registration authority, the newly established LLC is automatically registered as a taxpayer with local tax authorities and the State Pension Fund. The entire registration procedure takes a few days.

[87] There are no requirements regarding the minimum amount of the charter capital of an LLC, and thus it can be as small as UAH1. Participants must pay their charter capital contributions in full within six months of state registration unless otherwise envisaged by the LLC's charter.

[88] A participant in an LLC may transfer its ownership (participation) interest if it has obtained the consent of other participants, and only if it has first offered its participation interest to the other participants (in the proportions in which they hold their own interests), unless the pre-emptive right is waived by the provisions of the charter.

2.5 Corporate Governance in LLCs

[89] The corporate governance structure of an LLC consists of (i) a General Participants' Meeting (GPM); (ii) a Management Board; and (iii) a Supervisory Board (optional).

2.5.1 GPM

[90] GPM is the highest governing body of an LLC and has exclusive competence, *inter alia*, over the following matters:

- determination of the main objectives of the company;
- amendment to the company's charter and/or its charter capital;
- electing and dismissal of the executive body of the company, determining the amount of remuneration to the members of the executive body of the company;
- electing and dismissal of the members (certain members) of the Supervisory Board of the company, determining the amount of remuneration to the members of the Supervisory Board of the company;
- determining forms of control and supervision over the activity of the executive body of the company;
- approving the monetary valuation of a participant's non-monetary contribution;
- redistributing participation interests among the participants of the company in cases stipulated by law;
- forming other bodies of the company, determining the procedure for their activities;
- deciding on the company's purchase of the participation interest (a portion thereof) from a participant;
- approving the results of the company's activities for a year or another period of time;
- distribution of net profit of the company, deciding on payment of dividends;
- deciding on the spin-off, merger, de-merger, consolidation, liquidation and transformation of the company, electing the liquidation commission, approving the procedure for the termination of the company, the procedure for distribution of property remaining after the satisfaction of the creditors' claims among the company's participants in case of liquidation of the company, approving the liquidation balance sheet of the company;
- decisions regarding material responsibility claims against the company's officials;
- adoption of rules of procedure and other internal documents of the company, defining the organizational structure of the company;
- expulsion of a participant from the company.

[91] Issues attributed to the exclusive competence of the company's GPM may not be delegated to the company's Management Board.

[92] In general, decisions of an LLC's GPM require a simple majority vote of the LLC's participants. However, a decision on the following issues requires a vote of three-fourths of the total amount of votes of all the LLC's participants: (i) introducing changes and amendments to the charter of the company; (ii) change of the amount of charter capital; and (iii) deciding on the spin-off, merger, de-merger, consolidation, liquidation and transformation of the company, electing the liquidation commission, approving the procedure for the termination of the company, the procedure for distribution of property remaining after the satisfaction of the creditors' claims among the company's participants in case of liquidation of the company, approving the liquidation balance sheet of the company.

In addition, decisions must be taken unanimously by all participants of the company on the following matters: (i) approving the monetary valuation of a participant's non-monetary contribution; (ii) redistributing participation interests among the participants of the company in cases stipulated by law; (iii) forming other bodies of the company, determining the procedure for their activities; (iv) deciding on the company's purchasing the participation interest (a portion thereof) from a participant.

2.5.2 Management Board

[93] The Management Board is the executive body of an LLC. It is created in the form of a collegial body (board of directors) headed by a general director or sole authority (director). The Management Board decides on all issues of the company's activity except for issues that are under the exclusive competence of the GPM. A general director (director) may not preside at the meetings of the GPM.

[94] The Management Board (director) is accountable to the GPM and ensures the implementation of its decisions. It also acts on behalf of the company within the limits determined by the charter. The general director has the right to act on behalf of an LLC without a power of attorney. Other members of the Management Board may also be granted such right.

2.5.3 Supervisory Board

[95] The LLC can establish a supervisory board to control activities of its management body. The competence of the supervisory board should be determined in the LLC's charter.

[96] Ukrainian law does not contain any requirements or restrictions in relation to the members of the supervisory board of the LLC. Therefore, the members of the supervisory board may be Ukrainian or foreign citizens.

3 M&A ACTIVITY

3.1 Laws Affecting M&A

[97] The main laws governing M&A activity in Ukraine include the Civil Code, the Commercial Code, the Law on LLCs, dated 06 February 2018 (LLC Law), and the JSC Law. The LLC Law regulates activity of LLCs and additional liability companies. The JSC Law governs activity of JSCs. We note here that, in practice, the vast majority of cross-border M&A transactions involving Ukrainian companies are carried out pursuant to agreements governed by a law other than Ukrainian law, with English law being quite commonly used.

3.2 Forms of M&A Activity

[98] The Commercial Code provides that business entities may be established by the following means: incorporation of a new company, merger, adjoining (consolidation), division, separation and transformation.

[99] While we use the traditional term 'mergers and acquisitions' in this text, in practice statutory corporate mergers (which contemplate the aggregation of all rights and duties of two or more entities-predecessors resulting in the emergence of a new legal entity-successor and termination of the entities-predecessors) are very rarely used. Typically we have seen such mergers occur between companies within a single group of companies (for reasons of consolidation of operations, etc.).

[100] The most common types of M&A transactions in Ukraine include the following: (i) acquisition of shares (participation interests) under share purchase agreements; (ii) acquisition of assets under asset purchase agreements; (iii) mergers or adjoining two or more companies into one entity; (iv) issue of additional shares through a capital increase and acquisition of the new shares by a new shareholder (purchaser); and (v) formation of a new enterprise.

[101] Overall, the Ukrainian securities market is characterized by low levels of transparency, liquidity, efficiency and heavy regulation. The vast majority of mergers and acquisitions are carried out through private, not public transactions. Ukrainian law does not distinguish between friendly and hostile acquisitions, as the concept of a hostile transaction is not established by Ukrainian legislation. We note, however, that companies may be subject to 'raider' attacks, in which a competitor or other interested party attempts, in a hostile manner, to take over a company by various means, such as dubious lawsuits, and such attacks often exploit some previous defect in the company's corporate history or defects in title to key assets, etc.

3.3 Relevant Regulatory Authorities

[102] The main regulatory authorities relevant to M&A activity include the Securities Commission, the Anti-monopoly Committee of Ukraine (AMC) and the NBU (in respect of acquisitions in the banking sector).

[103] Due to relatively low thresholds for merger clearance, many cross-border M&A deals meet the requirements for obtaining prior AMC approval, the statutory timing for the issuance of which is usually forty-five days (with a simplified procedure, which lasts up to twenty-five days, can be applied in certain cases). In the event of the acquisition of at least 10% of the shares in a Ukrainian bank, in addition to the prior AMC approval, the purchaser will need to obtain the NBU's prior consent. NBU consent is deemed granted, if no refusal was issued by the NBU within three months from the date of the filing of all application documents.

[104] The filing process for obtaining regulatory approvals is typically handled by legal advisers, as it involves preparation and submission of an extensive package of documents, followed by additional document/ information requests from the regulators, correspondence and/or telephone discussions with the regulators to clarify their queries. Save for the AMC approval, the Ukrainian legislation does not envisage an expedited review procedure for obtaining regulatory approvals.

4 SPECIFIC ISSUES OF COMPANY/SECURITIES LAW

4.1 Shareholder Approval in Respect of M&A Transactions

[105] Mergers and acquisitions involving JSCs will typically require a shareholders' meeting (and potentially, super-majority approval) because during the acquisition the charter is likely to be amended and/or members of the board will be removed. Note, however, that approval of the transaction by the target is not required, though such approval requirement is most likely implicit in the requirement that shareholders approve charter changes and replacement of board members. The procedural formalities associated with such a meeting are discussed below.

4.1.1 JSCs

[106] With respect to JSCs, a transaction involving only a transfer of shares would probably not require shareholder approval absent proposed charter changes or removal of board members.

4.1.2 LLCs

[107] Mergers and acquisitions involving LLCs will often require a GPM. That is because the addition of a new participant to an LLC will, in the majority of cases, require amending its charter (in addition to any removal of board members).

4.2 Directors' Duties in M&A Transactions

[108] Ukrainian law imposes particular requirements on the company's management with respect to certain types of M&A transactions. In particular, the supervisory board is obliged to send out proposals of the new shareholder who has acquired more than 50% of the shares (controlling shareholding) in a JSC to all other shareholders offering to buy out their shares at a market value price within ten days after receipt of the relevant documents from the new shareholder.

[109] The law also provides for specific requirements and duties of the company management in the event of additional share issuance and reorganization by means of a merger, adjoining (consolidation), division, separation and transformation. Thus, the management of a JSC must notify the existing shareholders about their entitlement to exercise the right of first refusal during the additional share issue at least thirty days prior to such issuance.

[110] In case of the reorganization by means of a merger, adjoining (consolidation), division, separation and transformation, the Supervisory Board of each JSC taking part in such reorganization must provide the shareholders with the terms and conditions of the merger/adjoining (consolidation) agreement or division/separation/transformation plan and the written clarifications to such terms and conditions.

[111] A merger, adjoining (consolidation), division, separation, or transformation may not be completed before satisfaction of the creditors' claims. Within thirty days from the date of the GSM resolution regarding a merger, adjoining (consolidation), division, separation and transformation, the company management is required to send written notices to the company's creditors and publish the relevant statement in the official print media. Public JSCs must also inform each stock exchange where they are listed about their reorganization.

[112] Creditors whose claims to the JSC are not secured by any pledge or suretyship agreements may, within twenty days after the notification of termination of the company, require in writing that the JSC, in its sole discretion, perform one of the following actions: secure performance of its obligations by entering into a pledge or suretyship agreement, ensure early termination or performance of its obligations to the creditor and compensation for losses, unless the JSC and the creditor agreed otherwise. If the creditor has not made such written request within the specified term, any obligations of the JSC to such creditor are considered discharged.

4.3 Consideration for Shares

[113] JSC may place or sell shares it has repurchased at a price not less than its market value as approved by the supervisory board, other than in the course of: (i) establishment of the company; (ii) a merger, adjoining (consolidation), division, separation of the company.

[114] JSC has no right to place shares at a price less than their market value. The payment for shares is made by monetary funds or, if agreed between the JSC and the investor, by property and non-property rights or securities (other than debt equity securities issued by the acquirer and promissory notes). If consideration for shares is in the form of property, its value must correspond to the market value of such property as determined by an independent appraiser. The investor may not pay for securities by undertaking obligations to perform works or provide services to the company. Other restrictions with respect to the form of payment of securities may be established by the JSC charter.

4.4 Intellectual Property Rights

[115] Ukrainian IPR legislation provides protection, *inter alia*, to: copyright and neighbouring rights; trademarks and service marks; trade names; inventions; utility models; industrial designs; trade secrets; plant and animal varieties; appellations of origin; layouts of integrated circuits; and technical improvements.

[116] When acquiring IPR it is advisable to engage a patent attorney who will check the status of the registered IP and third party rights to it. Following the acquisition of the IP the new owner should register its property rights to the acquired intellectual property with the Ukrainian patent authorities. The registration process may vary in time from a fortnight to years depending on the type of intellectual property. Foreign companies and individuals are typically required to engage a patent attorney for the purpose of the registration of their IPR with the Ukrainian patent authorities.

[117] The value of intangible assets is usually set by the agreement of the parties. In the parties' discretion, the parties may seek independent appraisal by applying to the certified appraisers. If any conflicts arise in respect of the valuation, the parties may seek court resolution of such dispute.

4.5 Environmental or Product Safety Laws

[118] Environmental and product safety laws must be considered in case of the acquisition of companies, the activity of which is subject to regulation by various environmental or product safety laws. Such enterprises generally must obtain necessary licenses and permits, organize environmental management, conduct mandatory audits, adhere to specific requirements relating to the use of water and waste management, etc. It is important that legal consultants conducting the due diligence review of the respective target verify that all necessary licenses and permits have been secured by the target and are in good standing. It is also important to review the inspection reports issued by the regulators to find out about deficiencies/non-compliance in the activity of the target.

4.6 Completion Formalities

[119] M&A parties proceed to completion of a transaction subject to obtaining the required regulatory approvals, corporate authorizations and right of first refusal waivers of shareholders, where applicable. If an M&A transaction involves the sale of shares in a Ukrainian JSC, the share transfer is effected from the moment of the transfer of the shares from the seller's securities account to the buyer's securities account, which is evidenced by the extract from the buyer's securities account issued by the securities custodian. If an M&A deal involves the sale of the participation interest in a Ukrainian LLC, the transfer is deemed effective from the date of the registration of the new participant of the LLC with the Unified State Registry

of Legal Entities, Individual Entrepreneurs and Public Organizations. The shares sale and purchase agreements are not subject to mandatory notarization and may be executed in a simple form.

[120] The JSC Law sets certain obligations on the buyer concerned with the acquisition of substantial holdings of shares in a JSC: (i) a requirement to notify JSC and the Securities Commission about a buyer's intent to purchase 10% or more of the shares of a JSC (significant shareholding); and (ii) the obligation of a shareholder who has acquired more than 50% of the shares (controlling shareholding) to offer the remaining shareholders the option to have their shares purchased at a market value price.

4.7 Dividends

[121] Payment of dividends on ordinary shares must be carried out from the net profit for the accounting year and/or undistributed profit on the basis of a resolution passed by the GSM within the term not exceeding six months from the date of such resolution.

[122] Payment of dividends on preferred shares must be carried out from net profit for the accounting year and/or undistributed profit in accordance with the JSC charter within the term not exceeding six months from the end of the accounting year. In case of absence or insufficiency of net profit for the accounting year and/or undistributed profit of previous years, dividends on preferred shares are to be paid from a reserve capital or a special fund of the JSC.

[123] JSC may not pass a resolution on payment of dividends and pay dividends on ordinary shares if: (i) a share placement report has not been registered in accordance with the procedure established by law; (ii) the equity capital of the JSC is less than the total of its charter capital, reserve capital and the difference between disposal value of preferred shares and their nominal value; (iii) it owes obligations to its shareholders with respect to any mandatory share buy-back; (iv) current dividends on preferred shares have not been paid in full.

[124] JSC may not pass a resolution on payment of dividends and pay dividends on preferred shares if a share placement report has not been registered in accordance with the procedure established by law. Additionally, JSC has no right to pay dividends on preferred shares of a certain class unless current dividends on preferred shares have been paid to the holders who have priority with respect to receipt of dividends.

4.8 Purchase of Own Shares

[125] JSC is entitled, subject to GSM approval, to purchase shares from the consenting shareholders. The procedure for exercise of such right must be established in the charter of the JSC and/or by the GSM resolution. JSC may not approve a resolution on purchase of the shares if: (i) it owes obligations to its shareholders with respect to the mandatory share buy-back; (ii) JSC is or will become insolvent as a result of purchase of the shares; (iii) the equity capital of the JSC is or, as a result of such purchase, will become less than the total of its charter capital, reserve capital and the difference between disposal value of preferred shares and their nominal value.

[126] JSC shall have no right to purchase ordinary shares placed by it, unless current dividends on preferred shares have been paid in full, and has no right to purchase preferred shares placed by it, unless current dividends on preferred shares have been fully paid to the holders having priority with respect to receipt of dividends.

[127] JSC may not pass a resolution on purchase of shares without their cancellation if after such purchase the outstanding shares will constitute less than 80% of the charter capital of the JSC.

[128] Each holder of ordinary shares of the company is entitled to demand a mandatory buy-back of its shares by JSC if a relevant shareholder registered for participation in the GSM and voted against: (i) a merger, adjoining (consolidation), division, transformation, separation, change of type of the JSC; (ii) entering by JSC into a significant transaction or an 'interested party' transaction; (iii) change to the charter capital.

[129] JSC is required to pay for the shares repurchased from the shareholders within thirty days after receipt of the shareholder's demand for the mandatory buy-back, unless the parties agreed otherwise.

4.9 The Corporate Veil

[130] Ukrainian law does not contain any concept of piercing the corporate veil, which is found in Article 41 of the Ukrainian bankruptcy law.

4.10 Public Takeovers

[131] There is no specific law regulating public or private takeovers in Ukraine. The concept of hostile bids, in the Western sense of this term, is also undeveloped in the Ukrainian legal framework, particularly as the number of publicly traded companies is quite low. The general rules regarding mandatory buy-outs of shares from existing shareholders in the case of acquisitions of a majority shareholding (i.e., more than 50%) are discussed above.

4.11 Due Diligence Process

[132] Due diligence remains one of the most important steps of M&A transactions. The tendency in recent years shows that in smaller transactions buyers of businesses in Ukraine mostly prefer to carry out limited due diligence rather than the full scope reviews. As a result of such due diligence, legal and tax (audit) consultants typically issue a red-flag report which specifies the major issues and facts related to corporate, financial, tax, real estate, commercial, IP and IT matters of the target. Full-scale reviews generally are reserved for larger transactions. Competitive processes occur and appear to be on the rise in Ukraine as the level of cross-border M&A activity is steadily increasing.

[133] For the purpose of conducting due diligence, the seller typically arranges for a data room which contains originals or copies of documents with respect to the target prepared according to a request list prepared by the purchaser. In order to facilitate the due diligence process or in case of a bid for acquisition of the target in which several potential buyers participate, the data room is usually prepared in a virtual format. Such data rooms also provide the possibility to post questions and requests for additional information.

[134] As part of the due diligence review the seller is usually required to disclose, among others, all documents related to the target's establishment, corporate decisions and documents, licenses and permits (if any), material contracts, title documents to real estate owned or used by the target, regulators' inspection reports, and litigation documents involving the target. In addition to the documents disclosed by the seller, buyer's consultants usually obtain information relating to the target from the state registries and other public sources. Buyers typically also engage other advisors to carry out specific due diligence on tax, financial, commercial and technical matters, among others.

[135] When acquiring a target carrying out activity which may cause an environmental threat the due diligence review will generally include an environmental audit. Such audit may be conducted by the buyer (as part of the vendor's due diligence) or the seller. Vendor due diligence is becoming more common, even outside of a competitive tender process.

[136] The most common red flag issues which may be revealed during the due diligence of a Ukrainian target include deficiencies relating to title to assets, improper formation of the charter capital or lack of evidence of its due formation, incompliant corporate formalities, improper share transfers, labour law issues (e.g., salaries paid in envelopes), tax and compliance issues, violation of privatization process, use of unlicensed software, breach of environmental and anti-monopoly laws, etc. Some of these defects are due to specific conditions of conducting business in Ukraine.

[137] The due diligence helps to identify major problems which may negatively affect the target's activity, to negotiate the price and the scope of the warrantees and indemnities. The defects revealed during the due diligence could turn out to be very costly for the purchaser in the future, especially if some of them are incurable. In order for the purchaser to evaluate whether it wants to proceed with the acquisition, legal consultants distinguish between curable and incurable defects and estimate the risks of a negative outcome, as well as the time and cost to remove the faults or reduce risks. Buyer's legal counsel will also advise whether certain defects may be mitigated by addressing them in the warranties and indemnities in the sale and purchase agreement and/or introducing an escrow payment mechanism (holdback) providing for payment of the purchase price in instalments.

[138] As a matter of practice, transaction documents regulating cross-border M&A deals in Ukraine are often governed by English or other foreign law and the disputes which may arise from these deals are resolved by international arbitration or in foreign courts. Purely local transactions between Ukrainian counterparties are required to be documented under local law, with dispute resolution in Ukraine. We note that Ukrainian law in the area of mergers and acquisitions is not as commercially developed as in other jurisdictions, and customary concepts such as representations, warranties and indemnities have no distinct meaning under Ukrainian law (and, consequently, no direct consequences for a breach thereof).

4.12 Local Financing Options

[139] The Ukrainian capital market suffers from a lack of liquidity, and local financing for large-scale investments is often unavailable or insufficient, despite all political incentives implemented in recent years to address these issues. Interest rates on local borrowings, due to general stabilization of economy and relaxation of key policy rate by the NBU, approached the level of interest rates of other countries in the region, but still remain comparatively higher. As local debt financing is generally unaffordable and hard to obtain for the majority of the market participants, the more common source of financing for M&A deals remains equity financing and/or loans from foreign lenders (including international financial institutions and development finance organizations). In recent years, we have, in certain sectors (most notably in the renewable energy industry), witnessed such foreign loans being refinanced by local banks.

In February 2019, the Law of Ukraine 'On Currency and Currency Transactions' (the 'Currency Law') came into effect, which overhauled the previously (and somewhat restrictive) currency control regime in Ukraine. The Law is aimed at liberalization of the currency control regime in Ukraine, though the National Bank of Ukraine retains a vast amount of discretion in regulating foreign exchange. Since the adoption of the Currency Law, the National Bank of Ukraine adopted several regulatory acts, which liberalized Ukraine's currency control regime, and it continues to regularly liberalize the market with further measures.

[140] Due to the lack or insufficiency of domestic lending, Ukrainian companies actively seek foreign loans. Foreign entities acquiring Ukrainian companies are typically self-financed, meaning they obtain financing (if any) by using their established sources of financing in other countries. In recent years, most foreign financing in Ukraine has come from IFIs. Leveraged financing remains quite novel in Ukraine, and mezzanine financing from abroad is also rarely used. One noticeable benefit of the new currency control regime has been the cancellation of maximum interest rate caps on cross-border lendings. Instead, interest rates should now reflect market conditions, taking into account the NBU's recommendations. Pursuant to the Currency Law, the National Bank of Ukraine has the authority to reinstitute interest rate caps.

[141] The European Bank for Reconstruction and Development (EBRD) and the International Finance Corporation (IFC) have been active in Ukraine and offer a potential source of financing for investors into Ukraine, as well as other IFIs and DFIs. EBRD has focused its activities on investing in existing Ukrainian producers in conjunction with other multinational corporations. As such, EBRD may serve as a useful partner for potential investors interested in reducing their country-related risk in Ukraine. EBRD has been active in the telecommunications, agriculture, real estate, banking, retail and energy sectors, among others. IFC has also been active in many of these sectors.

[142] It is customary for banking loan and security agreements to contain 'change of control' clauses. If used, such clauses are generally enforceable in Ukraine.

[143] Ukrainian law contains very limited restrictions on using assets located in Ukraine to secure obligations of a non-Ukrainian borrower to a foreign creditor (e.g., state-owned assets not subject to privatization cannot serve as collateral, special procedure should be followed in respect of other state-owned assets in order they serve as a collateral).

5 SECURED FINANCING

[144] Where the acquisition is being financed by bank loans, the banks may obtain security either from the borrower itself or any third party surety (e.g., from members of the target group). Ukrainian law prohibits JSCs to issue loans for the purpose of the acquisition of their own shares or grant suretyships guaranteeing such loans.

[145] Secured financings in Ukraine may include:

- Mortgages over real property.
- Pledges over movable assets.
- Pledges over contractual rights/receivables.
- Pledges over rights to funds (e.g., bank accounts).
- Pledges over shares (for JSCs).
- Participatory interest pledges (for LLCs).
- Direct suretyships (corporates/individuals).
- Guarantees (banks/financial institutions).

[146] Collateral can be any property which may be alienated by the pledgor and which can be enforced against, including property which will be owned in the future. A security agreement must specify the key elements and the amount of the secured obligations, the term for their performance and details of the collateral sufficient to identify the collateral itself. The following may be included in the secured obligations: (i) the principal amount; (ii) interest and penalties on the principal amount; (iii) losses arising from a borrower's default; (iv) enforcement expenses; and (v) maintenance expenses relating to the disposal of the collateral.

[147] The concept of a 'floating charge' is broadly referred to in the notion of a Ukrainian law 'pledge of goods in circulation' or 'inventory pledge' which allows the pledgor to use the pledged assets and dispose of them in the ordinary course of the pledgor's business until an event of default. The pledgor retains the right to freely possess, use and dispose of the pledged goods, subject to special conditions agreed to in the pledge agreement. The pledge agreement needs to specify the type of pledged commodities and specify which commodities may be used for replacement of the initial collateral. Normally, the location of the pledged goods has to be identified in the pledge agreement. The pledgor, in case of disposal of goods, is obliged to replace them with other goods of the same or higher value. The pledgor may also replace the alienated goods with goods of lower value, subject to agreement.

5.1 Security Registration Requirements

5.1.1 Immovable Property

[148] All mortgages must be registered in the State Register of Proprietary Rights and Encumbrances over Real Property (Real Property Register). Registration is a condition to effectiveness of the mortgage agreement. Priority arises from the date of registration. The law also requires that mortgage agreements be notarized. Notably, the notaries certifying a mortgage agreement are authorized to make respective registration entries (including changes to the existing entries) in the State Register.

5.1.2 Movable Property

[149] Movable property pledge agreements may be registered with the State Register of Encumbered Movables (Encumbrances Register). The registration is not a condition to effectiveness of the pledge agreement, but if not registered, the pledgee's claim does not acquire priority against third parties or subsequently registered pledges. Registration is valid only for five years and must be updated periodically. Share pledges must also be reflected in the pledgor's securities account maintained by a custodian.

5.2 Security Enforcement

[150] Security interests created under security documents are enforced through court proceedings or pursuant to non-judicial procedures. In the case of court proceedings, a property is sold by auction (unless otherwise provided by an agreement or a court decision). Property of state-owned enterprises is sold exclusively by auction.

[151] The non-judicial procedures envisage the following means of pledge enforcement: (i) transfer of the pledged movable property to a pledgee; (ii) sale of the collateral through a sale-purchase agreement or at auction; or (iii) assignment of property rights and monetary claim rights to a pledgee.

[152] The pledgor is required to notify the borrower and other registered pledgees regarding an event of default and register such information with the relevant state register. Generally, a pledgor has a thirty-day grace period before the pledgee may start non-judicial enforcement, but if a delay in mortgage enforcement could cause damage to, destruction or loss of mortgaged property, a mortgagee is entitled to enforce the mortgage without prior notification.

[153] Funds received by the pledgee/lender from the sale of the pledged or mortgaged property must be distributed as follows: (i) as indemnity for expenses connected with the sale of the pledged property; (ii) satisfaction of secured demands of pledgees with higher priority; (iii) satisfaction of the pledgee's/lender's own secured demands; (iv) satisfaction of secured demands of pledgees with lower priority; and (v) refund the remaining to the borrower.

[154] Secured creditors' claims are satisfied at the account of a bankrupt's property as out-of-priority claims, including the claims of employees. The pledged/mortgaged property of the debtor in a bankruptcy proceeding should not constitute a part of liquidation estate and should serve only to satisfy the secured creditor's claims. The sale of the collateral in out-of-court enforcement results in termination of all existing secured indebtedness and, respectively, encumbrances securing such indebtedness. In the course of bankruptcy proceedings, sale of the collateral is likely to also render the secured obligations non-enforceable, though there is no stable practice on this matter.

6 ANTI-BRIBERY, ANTI-CORRUPTION AND ANTI-MONEY LAUNDERING LAWS AFFECTING M&A ACTIVITY

[155] Ukraine has long been known for its high level of corruption. In 2020 Transparency International ranked Ukraine 117th out of 180 countries in its Corruption Perception Index, which is a marginal improvement if compared with previous years. Despite the continuous public statements of Ukrainian politicians that combating corruption is a primary goal of Ukraine, and the pressure placed on the government by the World Bank, Western donor countries and other international organizations and IFIs, scarce steps have been taken in this direction.

[156] The main anti-bribery or anti-corruption laws which may affect M&A activity in Ukraine are the Law of Ukraine 'On Corruption Prevention' (Corruption Prevention Law or the Law) dated 14 October 2014, the Criminal Code of Ukraine dated 5 April 2001 (Criminal Code), the Code of Ukraine on Administrative Offences dated 7 December 1984 (Administrative Offences Code). These laws envisage criminal and administrative liability of various categories of individuals, including, *inter alia*, state and local governmental officials, officers and employees of private companies and individuals. Criminal Code also establishes liability of legal entities for corruption offences and allow courts to apply a fine in the amount of up to approximately USD60 000 or double the amount of the illegal benefit obtained by the legal entity. The law on whistleblowers (amendments to the Law), enacted in January 2020, introduces a reward and set of guarantees for individuals reporting corruption offences. The US Foreign Corrupt Practices Act (FCPA) and the UK Bribery Act which have an extraterritorial reach are also applicable and may affect M&A activity in Ukraine.

[157] The Corruption Prevention Law contains several provisions that should be taken into account during an M&A transaction. In particular, the Law requires private companies to implement a set of compliance measures. Moreover, management of a company should ensure regular assessment of corruption risks and undertake corresponding measures, etc. Failure to follow these requirements may result in cancellation of decisions in favour of a company, banning from public procurement and other negative consequences.

[158] In order to ensure proper enforcement of the anti-corruption laws, four anti-corruption authorities have been established. National Anti-Corruption Bureau of Ukraine (NABU) conducts investigations of corruption offences by high-ranking government officials, while Specialized Anti-Corruption Prosecutor's Office (SAPO) carries out public prosecution of investigated crimes in courts. National Corruption Prevention Agency is a preventive authority dealing with coordination of anti-corruption efforts and elaborating the country's anti-corruption policy. With the adoption of the Law of Ukraine 'On Supreme Anti-Corruption Court', in June 2018, Ukraine took a crucial step in accomplishing the institutional part of its anti-corruption reform. The Anti-corruption Court, which began work in September 2019, examines corruption cases investigated by NABU and SAPO.

[159] In December 2019, Ukraine also re-stated the Law of Ukraine 'On Prevention and Counteraction to Legalization (Laundering) of the Proceeds of Crime or Terrorist Financing' which provides for the updated legal framework for anti-money laundering. The new law aims to implement the respective EU regulations related to anti-money laundering into Ukrainian legislation. According to the law, all transactions which exceed the amount of UAH400 000 (approx. EUR12 000) are subject to mandatory financial monitoring by subjects of financial monitoring (e.g., banks) in Ukraine. The rules related to anti-money laundering regulation are also specified in the Criminal Code and various legal acts, including those related to regulation of the activity of the banks, financial companies and their clients. In 2017, a dedicated agency was established to deal with tracing, seizure and management of assets derived from corruption and other crimes. M&A activity in Ukraine must be conducted in compliance with the requirements of Ukrainian anti-money laundering legislation. Thus, such an ordinary action as the opening of bank or securities accounts in Ukraine is subject to financial monitoring and 'know your client' procedures.

7 FOREIGN INVESTMENT

7.1 Controls/Restrictions on Foreign Investment

[160] The laws regulating foreign investments in Ukraine include the Commercial Code, the Civil Code, the Law of Ukraine 'On Foreign Investment Regime', dated 19 March 1996 (Foreign Investment Law), the Law of Ukraine 'On Protection of Foreign Investments in Ukraine', dated 10 September 1991, and the Law of Ukraine 'On Investment Activity', dated 18 September 1991 (Investment Activity Law).

[161] As a general rule, Ukrainian legislation allows foreign investors to carry out business activities on the same basis, and with the same level of protection, as domestic investors. If Ukrainian legislation stipulates other rules in respect of the regulation of foreign investments than the provisions of applicable international treaties, the provisions of the latter shall prevail.

[162] Foreign investors conducting business in Ukraine have a variety of legal forms from which to choose. Business practice in Ukraine shows that JSCs and LLCs are the corporate structures most commonly used by foreign investors. Generally, Ukrainian law does not provide for any restrictions regarding the maximum permissible interest to be owned by a foreign investor subject to certain limitations addressed below.

[163] Ukrainian legislation sets out two categories of restrictions applicable to investment activity in Ukraine: (i) general restrictions relating to both domestic and foreign investors which envisage that certain types of activities must be carried out only by state-owned companies (e.g., armament, explosive production, rocketry industry, banknote production, blank forms of securities certificates); and (ii) specific restrictions applicable to foreign investors which envisage legally established maximum limits on the shareholding of foreign investors in the charter capital of Ukrainian companies doing business in a particular industry. The number of such industries is extremely limited. In particular, foreign investors are not allowed to hold more than 35% of shares in an information agency. Foreign investors are also restricted in establishing television and radio companies in Ukraine. In banking and financial services industries, foreign investors are subject to ancillary control under the specific banking and financial regulations. Some areas of business (i.e., licensed activities, privatization and public procurements) are restricted for business for investors originating from Russia, or controlled by such investors. In addition, foreign companies and individuals are prohibited by the Land Code of Ukraine dated 25 October 2001 (Land Code) from owning agricultural land but are entitled to own land designated for non-agricultural use.

[164] Ukrainian law sets no prohibition for hiring foreign directors or managers in Ukrainian companies, but they are subject to rules on employment of foreign nationals (*see* 'Employment Considerations' section). Ukrainian corporate legislation does not provide for any limitations with respect to the nationality of a person in a management position with a company as there are no provisions regarding obligatory presence of Ukrainian nationals in a management or supervisory board.

[165] To be functioning, a company must comply with the statutory requirements regarding permitting and licensing procedures. Although no special permit for a foreign investor to start business in Ukraine is required, permits and licenses may be required depending upon a company's contemplated area of activity. In many cases, as such permits or licenses can only be obtained by a Ukrainian company, a foreign company would only be permitted to conduct that activity by establishing a Ukrainian company (or acquiring a company with the relevant permits and licenses).

7.2 Incentives for Foreign Investment

[166] Foreign investors are entitled to the following protections and guarantees contained in the Foreign Investment Law:

- *Guarantees against changes to legislation affecting foreign investments. In the event that* Ukraine's legislation on foreign investments changes in any respect, foreign investments which are in operation prior to the change may continue to apply the benefits which were applicable under the law in effect when the investment was initially made, for a ten-year period after the effective date of the new legislation. However, these guarantees do not apply to changes in legislation relating to matters of defence, national security, enforcement of public order and environmental protection.
- *Guarantees against nationalization/expropriation and illegal actions of state bodies and officers.* The state of Ukraine and Ukrainian state bodies may not generally nationalize/expropriate foreign investments. Expropriation is permitted only in extraordinary cases, such as natural disasters, major accidents, human and animal epidemics, and may only be possible pursuant to the decisions of the state bodies authorized by the Cabinet of Ministers of Ukraine (Cabinet of Ministers).
- *Guarantees on compensation for loss and reimbursement of losses.* Foreign investors are entitled to be reimbursed for their losses, including lost profit and moral damages, caused by an act, omission or undue performance by Ukrainian state and local bodies and officers. If governmental or legislative acts violate

investors' rights, any losses incurred must be reimbursed in full by the respective state/legislative body. Reimbursement disputes are to be settled in courts.

- *Guarantees in the event of termination of investment activity.* Not later than six months from the termination of its foreign investment activity, a foreign investor is entitled to remit income and withdraw its investment and profits from such investment from Ukraine free from export duties.
- *Guarantees on transfer (repatriation) of profits.* After paying all applicable taxes, duties and other mandatory payments, foreign investors are guaranteed the unimpeded and immediate transfer abroad of their profits and foreign currency proceeds resulting from foreign investment in Ukraine, subject to Ukrainian currency exchange regulations.

[167] In addition to the above, the Investment Activity Law envisages the following guarantees to foreign and domestic investors:

- *Guarantees of stable investment conditions and observance of investor rights and legitimate interests.* The agreements signed by participants of investment activities remain valid for their duration, even when subsequent legislation establishes conditions which negatively affect the investor's status or restricts the investor's rights (with the exception of changes in tax, customs and currency legislation, or legislation relating to certain economic activities).
- *Guarantees on protection of investments, regardless of their ownership form.* Investors are entitled to an equitable regime which prevents state discrimination against investors and interference with administration, use and liquidation of an investment. State guarantees of investment protection may not be cancelled or restricted during the period of validity of such guarantees. State bodies and their officials may not interfere with any subject of investment activity except in accordance with law and within the authority of the given body and/or official.

On 13 February 2021, the Law of Ukraine No. 1116-IX 'On State Support for Investment Projects with Significant Investments in Ukraine' dated 17 December 2020 (the 'Support Law') entered into force. The Support Law aims to attract high-value foreign investment to Ukraine and defines the principal rules and guarantees for the implementation of investment projects (the 'investment project').

A Ukrainian or foreign investor can implement an investment project in the following industry sectors:

- Processing industry (except for the production and circulation of tobacco products, alcohol and alcoholic beverages)
- Extraction for the purpose of further processing and/or treatment of mineral resources (except for coal, oil and gas)
- Waste management
- Transport, warehousing
- Postal and courier activities, logistics
- Education, scientific and research and technical activities
- Healthcare
- Arts, culture, sports, tourism and resort and recreation.

An investment project can be carried out by means of providing construction, modernization, technical and/or technological re-equipment of the investment target, purchasing the necessary equipment and component parts thereto, and it can also provide for the construction of ancillary infrastructure facilities.

The investment project and the subsequent special investment agreement (the 'Agreement') shall comply with the following requirements:

- The amount of investment shall exceed EUR20 million.
- The implementation period of the investment project shall not exceed five years from the date of entering into the Agreement.
- The total value of the state support to implement the investment project shall not exceed 30% of the amount invested in the project.
- The investment project must create at least 80 new jobs, in which the average salary is at least 15% higher than the average salary paid for the relevant activity across the region.

Ukrainian state support of investment projects can take the following forms:

(1) Tax benefits such as: (i) exemption from customs charges and VAT for the equipment imported by an investor to Ukraine for implementation of the investment project and (ii) exemption of an investor from corporate income tax for five years.
(2) Exemption of equipment and component parts thereto from import duties.
(3) The right to use (lease) a state- or communally owned land plot in order to implement the investment project, as well as the investor's right to purchase that land plot upon the expiry of the term of the Agreement.
(4) The construction, at the expense of the state, of ancillary infrastructure facilities (motorways, communication lines, heat, gas, water and electricity supply facilities, utility supply lines) necessary to implement the investment project.

To apply for support for a qualifying investment project, the investor must submit an application and supporting documents to the special state body or local self-governmental authority (for regional projects). If the investment project is approved, the Cabinet of Ministers of Ukraine or the local council shall enter into the agreement that establishes the terms and conditions and the procedure for the project's implementation. The investment agreement can only be concluded with an investor that has a legal entity registered in Ukraine. If a foreign investor will implement the investment project, it needs to establish a legal entity in Ukraine with 100% of participation interests (shares) belonging to such foreign investors.

The government has a period of three to six months to consider the application and conclude the Agreement.

An application for the implementation of the investment project cannot be filed by:

(1) Ukrainian or foreign legal entities, which:

- are registered or controlled by residents of the Russian Federation or countries included in the FATF list;
- are subject to special economic or other restrictive measures (sanctions) in Ukraine;
- are undergoing bankruptcy proceedings, liquidation or reorganization;
- have tax arrears as of the date of the application;
- are registered in countries (or territories) classified as offshore zones.

(2) Non-profit enterprises, institutions, and organizations.
(3) State and municipal enterprises, in which more than 50% of shares (participation interests) in the charter capital are owned by the state or territorial community.

The Office of the President of Ukraine believes that this Law will help to resume investment activity in Ukraine after the pandemic related economic downturn that began in 2020.

7.3 Government Guarantees Against Expropriation or Nationalization

[168] As stated above, under Ukrainian foreign investment laws, expropriation is possible in extraordinary instances, such as natural disasters, accidents, human and animal epidemics, subject to provision of the relevant compensation to a foreign investor.

[169] A decision to expropriate may only be made by the Cabinet of Ministers. Ukraine guarantees adequate and effective compensation to foreign investors in the event of expropriation, as well as the right to repatriate all profits, provided they have been legally obtained.

[170] Any losses and damages suffered by foreign investors both as a result of expropriation and governmental acts must be compensated at current market prices and/or on the basis of a valuation confirmed by independent auditors. The compensation to be paid to a foreign investor shall be determined at the moment of termination of the property rights (in case of its expropriation) and at the moment of actual execution of a decision on compensation for losses (in case of an unlawful governmental act/omission).

[171] Compensation to a foreign investor must be quick, adequate and effective. Such compensation must be made in the currency that was used for the relevant investment or in any other currency acceptable to the foreign investor. From the moment the right to compensation arises, and up until the moment of its payment, interest shall be accrued on the amount of the compensation at the average rate of interest applied by London banks for granting of loans to first-class banks on the Eurocurrency market (LIBOR).

7.4 Currency Control and Licensing Regime

[172] Since its independence, Ukraine historically had relatively strict currency controls in place. As noted before, the Law 'On Currency and Currency Transactions' relaxed the currency control rules; however, some restrictions and limitations are still effective. These controls and restrictions are based on the general primary purpose of currency controls, that is, to regulate and prevent illegal capital outflows and maintain the stability of the national currency. Some of the more fundamental restrictions have been in place for over twenty years. Others have been enacted over time (and are periodically revised). Some are 'situational' and are implemented for temporary periods in response to particular circumstances affecting the stability of the foreign exchange market and/or the stability of the national currency. These latter measures were onerous for businesses, as well as for banks, which are often required to implement them in practice and monitor compliance therewith.

On 7 February 2019, Ukraine overhauled its currency control regime by way of implementing a new currency control legislative framework, including the Currency Law and a number of regulations of the National Bank of Ukraine implemented pursuant to the Currency Law. The Currency Law sets out the fundamental principle of freedom of currency transactions, unless expressly prohibited by law (in contrast to the former approach – currency transactions are prohibited, restricted and/or require specific authorization/license, unless a specific exemption applies). Notwithstanding the above, there are still a number of restrictions related to currency transactions.

[173] For example, any cross-border transfer of funds (save for certain exemptions) by a Ukrainian resident legal entity is limited to the aggregate amount of EUR2 000 000 per year (or in equivalent in other currencies) (the 'Limitation Amount'). The same approach is also applicable to individuals, who are residents of Ukraine (cross-border transfer of funds by such individuals is limited to the aggregate amount of EUR100 000 per year). The Limitation Amount applies to all cross-border transactions of Ukrainian resident – legal entities irrespective of the number of counterparties. The Limitation Amount, among other exemptions, is not applicable to own operations of Ukrainian banks, including state-owned banks and payments for import and export of services.

[174] The main regulatory basis for regulation of currency operations is the Resolution of the National Bank of Ukraine No. 5 dated 02 January 2019 'On Approval of Regulation on Anti-Crisis Measures and Procedure for Carrying Out of Certain Foreign Currency Transactions', as well as the other regulations of the NBU, supplementing the Resolution No. 5.

[175] The main regulated currency operation in Ukraine is the transfer of currency assets from Ukraine. Currency assets are defined broadly to not only include cash and cash equivalents but also banking metals, securities and other payment documents with a 'face value'.

[176] Residents and non-residents fall under the regulation of different legal regimes with regards to currency legislation, due to which, e.g., foreign investment into Ukraine by non-residents is generally to be made only in foreign currency. Residents, on the other hand, are restricted in their ability to freely transfer currency abroad, which exceed the limits for such transfer, save for some exceptions (e.g., repayment of debt to foreign creditors, transfer or currency related to fulfilment of obligations under collateral, own operations of banks).

[177] Ukrainian companies acquired by foreign investors are treated as resident entities and are subject to the same limitations imposed on residents when sending hard currency to their parent companies or other entities abroad (save for repatriations of dividends, which are not subject to the limitations).

7.4.1 Currency Exchange Issues

[178] At this writing, the timeframe for settlements under export/import contract is 365 calendar days. Additionally, proceeds of Ukrainian residents from export operations must be transferred to an account in a Ukrainian bank. Over the years, Ukraine has often vacillated between a 90-day and a 180-day settlement period for export-import operations, but since liberalization of the currency control regime, the National Bank of Ukraine has been keen to ease this requirement.

7.4.2 Financing by Non-residents

[179] With respect to financing of Ukrainian residents by non-residents, since 2019 mandatory registration of loan agreements with the NBU prior to receiving the actual financing has been abolished. Instead, servicing banks should notify the NBU about the executed cross-border loan agreements before effecting any payments outside Ukraine. In case of any amendments to such cross-border loan agreements, servicing banks shall make the respective entries within the special informational system of the NBU.

[180] While since 2019 interest rate caps for cross-border loans have been cancelled, according to the NBU's guidelines, servicing banks should take into account the following indicators when assessing the interest rate on such loans: (i) the cost of financing, established on world markets (e.g., LIBOR, loan rates of central banks of other countries, where the lender is registered); (ii) the margin, which should correspond to the sovereign risk rate of Ukraine and the individual risk rate of a particular borrower; and (iii) interest rates under sovereign Eurobonds of Ukraine (for intra-group loans).

[181] The National Bank gradually simplified currency control restrictions and limitations during 2019–2020 and periodically continues to further relax existing limitations.

7.5 Currency Regulation and Foreign Investment

[182] Current Ukrainian legislation allows without any limitations repatriation of investment and dividends for foreign investors.

[183] According to applicable legislation monetary investments may be carried out in UAH or foreign currencies. To conduct monetary investments a non-resident should open in its name an account (investment, current, escrow or correspondent) in a Ukrainian bank. An investor has the right to sell foreign currency that was properly credited to its bank account and use the funds in UAH obtained from such sale for investment purposes.

[184] According to banking regulations resident and foreign investors have the right to purchase and exchange foreign currency for purposes of returning (repatriating) income (dividends), profits and other funds received from their investment activity in Ukraine. To purchase currency for these purposes, the foreign investor or the resident paying the amount to the foreign investor might be asked for documentation by the servicing bank in order to substantiate that the investment had been properly made and/or to substantiate the proper entitlement to the income/proceeds of that investment. These documentation requirements vary for different types of investments, such as in respect of direct investments, portfolio investments in securities, portfolio investments in government bonds, other types of investment activity, investment deposits (in banks), and joint activity (e.g., an unincorporated joint venture). For example, for payments in respect of direct investments (such as shares of a bank), the documentation would include (where relevant), a copy of an investment contract, a copy of a contract for joint activity, bank statements evidencing that the investment had indeed been made into Ukraine, a copy of the foundation documents of the company in which the investment was made, a copy of the tax declaration from the company in which the investment was made which confirms that the company has profits to distribute, a copy of a tax certificate confirming the payment of any taxes due by the non-resident in respect of the income being repatriated (or a certificate confirming that pursuant to a relevant double tax treaty no tax is to be withheld), a copy of the resolution of the shareholders of the company regarding the liquidation of the company or dividends distribution, etc. If the investment was properly made at the outset, these requirements are generally not difficult to comply with and do not result in delays in repatriating investment-related income or proceeds.

[185] If a foreign investor were to attempt to exit as a shareholder or participant in a Ukrainian company, whether by means of a sale of its shares or participation interest to a Ukrainian resident or by deciding to exit as a participant (or decreasing the company's capital), the investor would, in such case, likely only be able to receive proceeds in UAH, which, however, further could be converted into foreign currency and repatriated abroad through the investor's bank account (either from an investment account, current, or any other account).

[186] Despite the fact that the NBU relaxed/cancelled several currency control restrictions and limitations, a number of restrictions in respect of cross-border transactions remain, which potentially might affect the operations of a Ukrainian company.

8 MERGER CONTROLS: ANTITRUST/ COMPETITION ISSUES

8.1 Relevant Legislation and Competent Authorities

[187] The legal framework for Ukraine's merger control regime is set out in the Law of Ukraine 'On Protection of Economic Competition' dated 11 January 2001 (Competition Law). The Competition Law regulates, *inter alia*, merger control issues, introduces the concept of a 'concentration', establishes the economic thresholds, exemptions and sanctions and provides for basic filing requirements, review procedures and conditions for granting approvals for a concentration (Approval for Concentration). The Regulation 'On the Procedure for Submitting Applications to the AMC for Obtaining Prior Approval for Concentration of Entities' (approved by Order No. 33- of the AMC), dated 19 February 2002 (Concentration Regulation), envisages the filing requirements for obtaining Approvals for Concentration in more detail.

[188] The Anti-Monopoly Committee of Ukraine (AMC) is the entity responsible for the enforcement of laws relating to antitrust and anticompetitive activities. The AMC carries out this task primarily by reviewing proposed transactions for their anticompetitive effects and makes decisions on granting of the Approvals for Concentration.

[189] The Cabinet of Ministers may act in the capacity of the AMC as an authority authorized to review proposed transactions and to grant Approvals for Concentration. Thus, if the AMC has not approved certain transaction, the participants to a concentration are entitled to file an application to the Cabinet of Ministers for obtaining an Approval for Concentration. The Cabinet of Ministers may approve the concentration if its participants can show that the positive social effects of the concentration outweigh the negative consequences of the restriction of competition.

[190] Complex transactions aimed at the acquisition of several targets in different jurisdictions, or where the target and the acquirer are active in other overlapping markets outside of Ukraine, may also require approvals of other relevant authorities authorized to grant such approvals in those jurisdictions, including the European Commission.

8.2 Concentrations

[191] The Ukrainian merger control regime provides for pre-merger filings. This means that the contemplated concentration must not be put into effect prior to obtaining clearance from the AMC.

[192] The following transactions are considered as a concentration and may be subject to prior merger clearance:

(1) merger or consolidation of business entities;
(2) acquisition of direct or indirect control over a business entity or over a part of a business entity, *inter alia*, by way of:
  - purchase, lease, obtaining in management or in use of assets of a business entity;
  - appointment to management positions, including the chairman, deputy chairman of the supervisory board, management board, or of another supervisory or executive body, appointment of the CEO, deputy CEO of individuals who already hold similar positions in other business entities, appointment of more than 50% of the positions in the supervisory board, management board, or another supervisory or executive body of a business entity of the same individuals who already hold these positions in other business entities;
(3) establishment by two or more business entities of an entity (e.g., a joint venture) that will be independently engaged in business activities for an extended period of time;
(4) direct or indirect acquisition, obtaining ownership of, or management over, the shares (participation interest) of the business entity, if such acquisition results in obtaining 25% and more or 50% and more of the voting rights in the highest governing body of the target business entity.

[193] If a transaction qualifies as a 'concentration', then the Approval for the Concentration must be sought if the following thresholds are met:

- the aggregate value of assets or aggregate sales turnover of the goods of participants to the concentration, taking into account relations of control, in the preceding financial year, including outside of Ukraine, exceeded EUR30 million, *wherein* the value (aggregate value) of assets or sale turnover (aggregate turnover) in Ukraine of at least two participants to the concentration, taking into account relations of control, each exceeded EUR4 million; *or*
- the aggregate value of assets or sale turnover of goods in Ukraine of the undertaking with respect to which control is being acquired or the undertaking whose assets, shares (equity interest) are being acquired into ownership or obtained management or for use, or of at least one of the founders of the undertaking being created, taking into account relations of control, in the preceding financial year, exceeded EUR8 million, *wherein* the sales turnover of goods of one other participant in the concentration, taking into account relations of control, in the preceding financial year, including outside of Ukraine, exceeded EUR150 million.

[194] Article 2 of the Competition Law provides that 'This Law applies to relationships that have or may have an impact on economic competition in the territory of Ukraine.'

The Competition Law does not clarify what should be understood as 'transactions that affect or may affect economic competition in the territory of Ukraine', and there is no relevant case law in this regard. The informal (undocumented) position of the Ukrainian competition authority is that any concentration, which meets the established financial thresholds, may affect economic competition in the territory of Ukraine, and therefore must be approved by the AMC.

8.2.1 Who Is a 'Participant' in a Concentration?

[195] The term 'participants' to the concentration is very wide, and includes direct participants (parties) to the concentration and all entities and individuals connected with them by control relations.

Direct participants to the concentration are:

- a merger: the entities involved in the merger;
- an acquisition of stakes, assets in an entity, obtaining of assets in lease, management or use: the undertaking acquiring the stakes, assets in a company, obtaining the assets in lease, management or in use and the entity in which the stakes, assets are acquired, which provides the assets in lease, management or in use;
- an establishment of a new entity: the founders of such entity; and
- an acquisition of control: the undertaking acquiring control and the entities over which control is being acquired.

[196] Participants to the concentration also include all entities and individuals who are connected by control relations with the direct participants (parties) to the concentration. In this context an undertaking is connected by control relations if it either controls, or is controlled by, one of the direct participants, or is controlled by the undertaking that controls one of the direct participants. Again, the definition of 'control' is broad, and includes any ability (either solely or jointly with any other undertakings) to perform decisive influence over business activity of an entity. 'Control' also includes the notion of affiliated individuals (family members). All such undertakings that are connected by control relations are considered to be one group of undertakings.

[197] The practical effect of this broad definition of 'participant' includes the fact that where an actual participant is a member of a corporate group (e.g., seller's and target's group, or buyer's group), the asset value/turnover and market share of the entire group should be used to calculate whether the thresholds are reached. Moreover, the financial data of the seller's group needs to be taken into account even if the control relations between the seller and the target will cease upon closing of the contemplated transaction.

[198] In many cases, a large number of entities and persons will be deemed to be 'participants' in the relevant concentration under Ukrainian law, and the thresholds will be exceeded even where the participants' individual presence in, or connection to, Ukraine is minimal. Thus, as noted above, the requirement for obtaining prior Approval for Concentration often extends to purely foreign deals, i.e., those carried out outside Ukraine, if the relevant parties have a certain nexus to Ukraine, such as having Ukrainian subsidiaries or sales to Ukraine, regardless of the concentration's actual impact on competition in Ukraine, if the formal requirements for obtaining Approval for Concentration are otherwise met.

8.2.2 Process/Mechanics

Pre-notification Procedure

[199] Formally, applicable Ukrainian merger control regulations do not envisage a Pre-notification Procedure as a stage of the review process. According to the Concentration Regulation, the parties to the concentration when filing the application to the AMC are entitled to request preliminary consultations with the AMC regarding the scope of information required for the filing, and curing any defects of the application during the preview period. Though formally such procedure is envisaged at the stage when a merger application is filed, in practice, the AMC informally states that such consultations can be requested by the parties before the actual filing of the application.

[200] The scope of information to be disclosed in the application depends on whether the concentration is subject to a simplified or regular procedure of review. The simplified procedure may be applied if:

- only one participant to the concentration carries out its activities in the territory of Ukraine; or
- the aggregate market share of participants to the concentration in the same market does not exceed 15%; or
- the market shares or aggregate market shares of the participants to the concentration do not exceed 20% of the market where products (goods, works, services) are sold without acquisition or sale of which the business activity of any other participant to the concentration becomes impossible.

Considering the definition of participants to the concentration, as described above, the sellers' group must be taken into account even if control relations with the target group cease upon completion of the concentration. In all other cases, the regular procedure of review is applied.

However, if the AMC considers that the filing should be reviewed under the regular procedure instead of the simplified procedure, it is entitled to make such a decision and apply the regular review procedure.

[201] Under the regular procedure the application must be accompanied mainly with the following documents and information:

- participant's group charts showing control relations before and after the concentration;
- extensive and substantiated economic rationale for the transaction, including comprehensive competition assessment and market shares estimation;
- 'Information on Concentration' containing information on beneficial owners of the participants in the concentration and their affiliates registered and/or operating in Ukraine, description of control relations among the participants, their beneficial owners and said affiliates, confirmation that the participants to the concentration do not include any entities or individuals that are under any sanctions according to the laws of Ukraine, description of the business activity of the participants and their affiliates, description of the

concentration including financial aspects (the price and sources of financing of the transaction);
- calculation of the financial thresholds of the participants to the concentration;
- copies of the documents confirming the financial aspects of the concentration (sources of financing the concentration);
- documents confirming the legal status of the participants;
- applicable transaction documentation (e.g., sale-purchase agreements, shareholder agreements);
- document confirming payment of the filing fee.

[202] Under the simplified procedure the application must be accompanied with the following documents and information:

- information on direct participants to the concentration, their controlling entities up to the individuals – beneficial owners and any entities of the group registered and/or operating in Ukraine (affiliates), description of control relations among them, confirmation that the participants to the concentration do not include any entities or individuals that are under the sanctions according to the laws of Ukraine, description of the business activity of the participants and their affiliates, description of the concentration including financial aspects, the financial thresholds of the participants, information about relevant markets in Ukraine, including market shares of the participants for the last two years and for the reporting period of the current year, short description of economic rationale for the transaction;
- participant's group charts showing control relations before and after the concentration;
- copies of the documents confirming the financial aspects of the concentration (sources of financing the concentration);
- documents confirming the legal status of the participants;
- applicable transaction documentation (e.g., sale-purchase agreements, shareholder agreements);
- motion to consider the application under the simplified procedure;
- document confirming payment of the filing fee.

[203] In case the application does not contain information about beneficial owners of the participants to the concentration (or in case there are no such beneficial owners – an explanation why there are none), the AMC bounces the application back and the parties may re-submit it including the required information about beneficial owners.

[204] In case, the participants to the concentration include any entities or individuals that are under sanctions that, according to the laws of Ukraine, forbid the respective transaction, the AMC rejects the application without any review,

[205] The preparation of the approval application package can be time-consuming, but will depend on how quickly the applicants can compile the necessary information. The application itself is required to be in Ukrainian, and certain documents (including foundation documents, certificates of incorporation, powers of attorney), if generated abroad, will need to be apostilled (legalized) and also translated into Ukrainian.

[206] Once the application package has been completed it can be submitted to the AMC for review, along with a fee payment certificate. The filing fee amounts to UAH20 400 (approx. USD730) for the review of the application. The application package may be submitted by legal advisers or other representatives of the participants to the concentration based on the respective power of attorney. These representatives will be the contact persons of the participants to the concentration during the review process.

Procedure for Assessment and Approval/Rejection of a Concentration

[207] The simplified notification procedure shall last up to twenty-five calendar days. A 'simplified' application may be returned by the AMC if it does not fall within the criteria for the application to be considered under the simplified procedure, or if the AMC based on any other grounds will decide that the application should be reviewed based on the regular procedure. To decide on this (and either to accept or reject the application) the AMC has fifteen calendar days after submission.

[208] The regular notification procedure normally takes up to forty-five calendar days, which include 15 (fifteen) calendar days for an initial review to determine whether the application package complies with all of the AMC's formal requirements (Preview period) and 30 (thirty) calendar days to review the application in substance (Phase I review).

If the 'regular' application package complies with all of the AMC's formal requirements, it is deemed to be accepted by the AMC for review after expiration of fifteen calendar days. If the AMC determines that the application materials are not in compliance with its requirements, the AMC will be entitled to return the package for curing the application's defects, which will restart the application's review period.

Following a fifteen-day preview period, the AMC then has thirty calendar days to review the application in substance. If the AMC does not render a decision within this term, the approval is considered to be granted at the expiration of the forty-five-day period. However, in practice the AMC does not allow the situation when the approval is granted based on tacit consent, and always passes formal decision.

If, during the Phase I review period, the AMC reveals that the concentration may lead to monopolization of the market, it can open a Phase II investigation. The AMC should then complete such investigation within 135 calendar days from the date of notice to the applicants on initiating the Phase II investigation. Information on initiating of the case investigations (Phase II) is published on the website of the AMC.

Also if during the Phase I review the AMC will scrutinize historical transactions of any of the parties and discover an earlier failure (by any of them) to obtain Approval for Concentration for an earlier transaction (if such approval was required), the AMC can delay granting Approval for the current transaction until the decision in the case initiated by the AMC with respect to the previous violation is taken. Any decisions on such cases can include the imposition of a fine by the AMC on the respective party and a requirement that the violating party obtain a post-closing Approval for Concentration for the prior (unapproved) transaction.

[209] When reviewing the application package the AMC analyses the impact of the proposed concentration on the relevant market(s) and the respective market players, taking into account, *inter alia*, potential increase of the market shares of the participants as a result of the proposed concentration. Thus, if upon such examination, the AMC makes a decision that the concentration will not lead to the monopolization of, or a significant restriction of competition on, the relevant market the Approval for Concentration should be granted. If the AMC finds grounds to prohibit the concentration it shall notify the parties to such concentrations and give them thirty days to propose remedy obligations mitigating or removing the negative impact of such concentration on competition. Remedy obligations may be either structural (e.g., divestment of some assets) or behavioural (e.g., a prohibition of unjustified price increases, decrease of production volume). Remedy obligations are not comprehensively regulated by the laws and may be negotiated with the AMC and established on a case-by-case basis provided that such obligations are proportional to and justified by the anticompetitive threats of the transaction.

[210] Because obtaining the Approval for Concentration is both a relatively lengthy process as well as being a pre-requisite to effecting a concentration, unless the application process is properly managed from the outset, there can be a significant delay before a transaction can be completed. In addition, completion of transactions subject to an Approval for Concentration is generally conditioned upon such approval having been obtained to the satisfaction of the buyer. The procedures and relevant time frames described above should thus be taken into account when determining a long-stop date by which the transaction should complete.

Sanctions for Failure to Obtain the Approval for Concentration

[211] A concentration carried out without the prior Approval for Concentration in circumstances where such approval was required may result in a fine amounting up to 5% of the aggregate annual revenue of the participant to the concentration for the previous reporting year. Exact amount of the fine is estimated by the AMC according to its Recommendatory Guidelines on Calculation of Fines for Violations of the Competition Legislation dated 9 August 2016 ('Guidelines'), and normally is imposed over the acquiring party. The Guidelines set forth a transparent methodology to be used by the AMC for calculating amounts of fines being imposed for violations of the Ukrainian competition legislation.

Based on these Guidelines the amount of fine for failure to obtain prior Approval for the Concentration can comprise the amount:

- between UAH170 000 and UAH510 000 (approx. USD6 300 and USD18 900) in case the parties are active on non-overlapping and non-adjacent markets in Ukraine;
- between UAH510 000 (approx. USD18 900) and 5% of the turnover on the relevant and on adjacent markets in case the concentration does not lead to

monopolization or significant restriction of competition and/or has no impact on Ukrainian product markets;
- 10% of the turnover on the relevant and on the adjacent markets in case the concentration resulted in monopolization or substantial restriction of competition in Ukraine.

The limitation period for imposition of a fine comprises five years after the date of the concentration.

[212] Moreover, if such concentration results in a monopoly or a significant restriction of competition on the relevant market or a part thereof, then the AMC may launch court proceedings seeking to invalidate the relevant transaction agreements.

[213] Additionally, individuals and companies who have suffered losses as a result of the breach of anti-monopoly legislation may file a claim seeking compensation of damages. Such losses shall be compensated in an amount equal to double the amount of losses suffered by the claimant.

The full version of the AMC decision on imposition of a fine (except for any confidential information) is published on the AMC's official website, including description of the violation, names of the parties involved, amount of a fine imposed. Information on the biggest fines regularly appears in mass media. Therefore, the parties should also consider reputational risks connected with failure to obtain prior Approval for Concentration.

As described above, failure to obtain prior Approval for Concentration can also delay any future Approvals of the AMC. If the AMC discovers an earlier failure to obtain Approval for Concentration (if it was required), it may delay granting Approval for Concentration on any new transaction until the decision in the case initiated with respect to the previous violation is taken. Within such a process on a violation, the AMC can impose a fine on the respective party (unless the limitation period has expired) and require obtaining a post-closing Approval for Concentration.

[214] In the case of the abuse of the monopoly position on the relevant market, the AMC may rule on the forced division of that enterprise.

Preliminary Conclusion of the AMC

[215] It is possible for a participant to a concentration to seek a preliminary conclusion from the AMC as to whether or not (i) it is necessary for the participants to file an application in respect of a specific transaction (e.g., in circumstances where it is unclear if the filing requirements are met); and (ii) it is likely that the AMC will give its approval to a particular transaction. The AMC charges a processing fee of UAH5 440 (approx. USD200) in respect of these preliminary rulings and has a month to review and process such an application. If the AMC, however, comes to the conclusion that its approval is required to permit the proposed concentration, the parties must then file the application to the AMC with all the required documents (except documents which were filed for the preliminary review), which may take either twenty-five or forty-five days for the AMC to review, as discussed above.

Therefore, contracting parties often choose to voluntarily make a full application to the AMC to avoid the risk of being subject to a lengthier process.

8.3 Anticompetitive Restraints

[216] Ukrainian legislation sets out a number of activities which are capable of being classified as anticompetitive.

8.3.1 Concerted Practices

[217] Pursuant to the Competition Law concerted practices are essentially any actions of a competitive nature that are agreed by two or more business entities. There are two types of concerted practices, i.e., those that are prohibited (anticompetitive concerted practices) and those that can be allowed subject to obtaining respective approval of the AMC.

[218] Under the Competition Law any concerted practice between entities which has led or could potentially lead to the prevention, elimination or restriction of competition is considered anticompetitive and is prohibited. Anticompetitive concerted practices include: (i) price-fixing; (ii) market division; (iii) restriction of market access; (iv) distortion of the results of tenders and auctions; (v) substantial restriction of competitiveness of other entities without justification; and (vi) entering into agreements that are conditional on the contracting party's acceptance of additional obligations which are unrelated to the subject matter of an agreement. The prohibition applies equally to actions which are the result of vertical or horizontal arrangements. The actions need not necessarily result from formal agreements and may be based on informal arrangements and concerted practices.

[219] In certain cases, concerted practices can be approved by the AMC, for example, (a) if the participants can prove that the relevant practices encourage manufacturing, technological or economic development, or the development of small or medium-sized enterprises; and (b) if the practices do not lead to a substantial restriction of competition on the market. In addition, in certain circumstances, the Cabinet of Ministers has the right to allow concerted practices (even where the AMC has not approved such practices) if the participants can show that the positive social effects of these practices outweigh the negative consequences of the restriction of competition. There are currently no criteria for measuring such positive effects.

[220] The AMC's requirements to concerted practices contain exemptions from the requirement to obtain the AMC approval, i.e., the parties may be exempted from obtaining the AMC approval (i) if their aggregate market share is less than 5% of the relevant market; or (ii) if their aggregate market share is less than 15% (for horizontal and combined concerted actions), 20% (for conglomerate concerted actions) or 30% (for vertical concerted actions) of the relevant market, as long as certain other criteria are met; or (iii) in certain circumstances where the parties are small or medium-sized enterprises.

[221] As part of an M&A deal, the parties often enter into various restrictive covenants, such as an obligation of the seller not to compete with the target for a certain period of time after closing, so as to ensure that the target's trade secrets, business connections and practices are preserved and the buyer is entitled to a maximum return on its investment. These restrictive covenants are as a rule limited by time and territory. As a matter of practice, the AMC approval for concerted practices is generally issued for the period not exceeding three years. As a practical matter, the effectiveness of such restrictive covenants, when included in a sale purchase agreement for an M&A transaction, are conditioned upon AMC approval being obtained, but such approval is generally not included as a condition to closing. Parties typically file both applications to the AMC (for a concentration and for concerted practices) simultaneously, but then proceed to closing once the concentration approval has been obtained (whilst the concerted practices approval is pending).

[222] Agreements on the sale and purchase of a business often contain restrictions aimed at non-solicitation of the key employees by the previous owners. Even though such provisions are frequently used in M&A deals, they may be successfully challenged in Ukrainian courts as such which restrict the constitutional right of Ukrainian citizens to choose their place of employment.

[223] Entities wishing to obtain approval from the AMC in respect of concerted practices must prepare an application package, and in this case, the AMC has 3.5 months to decide whether or not to authorize the concerted practices (which is longer in comparison to Approval for Concentration which normally takes up to 45 calendar days). The AMC charges a processing fee of UAH10 200 (approx. USD365) for the review of the application.

[224] As is the case in relation to concentrations (referred to above), it is possible for an entity to seek clarification from the AMC as to (i) whether or not a certain activity qualifies as a concerted practice; and (ii) in cases where an activity does qualify as a concerted practice, to seek a preliminary conclusion from the AMC as to whether or not the AMC is likely to give its consent to such concerted practice. The AMC charges a processing fee of UAH5 440 (approx. USD195) in respect of each of these preliminary conclusions.

8.3.2 Penalties

[225] Where anticompetitive concerted practices are found to exist, the AMC may impose fines on an undertaking of up to 10% of its turnover for the previous financial year.

[226] The fine for concerted practices performed without the AMC approval (if such was required), the AMC may impose a fine over an undertaking of up to 5% of its turnover for the previous financial year.

[227] In addition, individuals and companies who have suffered losses as a result of anticompetitive concerted practices or concerted practices performed without prior AMC approval (if such was required) may file claims seeking compensation

for their damages. Such losses shall be compensated in double amount of losses suffered by the claimant.

9 TAXATION ASPECTS

9.1 Nature of the Tax Regime

[228] Ukraine's taxation system continues its development and remains relatively complex. The tax laws are amended often and sometimes retrospectively. They are still characterized by lack of precise policy or explanation. A number of government bodies and different levels of the state tax authorities issue their own interpretations of tax legislation which may be contradictory. Many issues still remain open for clarification. All these factors lead to the risk of a different interpretation of tax legislation by the state tax authorities and taxpayers.

[229] In 2011, Ukraine's first Tax Code, dated 2 December 2010 (Tax Code), came into force and consolidated many Ukrainian tax laws into one document, eliminated ineffective taxes, and introduced a number of important changes into the taxation system in order to simplify and update it.

[230] In 2019, the Cabinet of Ministers of Ukraine reformed the State Fiscal Service of Ukraine into two separate bodies: State Tax Service and State Customs Service. This was done with the objective of achieving: a decrease in the number of taxes, simplification of administration of taxes, a decrease in the tax burden on salaries, and tax decentralization. The main goal was to simplify tax administration and motivate businesses to conduct business transparently and make Ukraine more attractive for investment purposes.

[231] Recent novelties relate to the Organization for Economic Cooperation and Development (OECD) base erosion and profit shifting (BEPS) requirements. Anti-BEPS Law entered into force in May 2020, and it establishes new tax reporting procedures of principal purpose tax, new narrowed concept of a beneficial owner for the purposes of double tax treaties, new taxation requirements for permanent establishments, taxation of alienation of Ukrainian real estate rich companies, new tax rules for non-residents, amends transfer pricing rules and principles of accounting and tax adjustments, etc.

9.2 Liability to Tax

[232] Ukraine domestic tax law considers all legal entities as opaque. The income derived at the level of such entity is only taxed in the hands of the entity rather than being attributed to the owners or shareholders that are 'behind' the entity.

[233] The notion of a domestic entity for tax purposes is included in the definition of residency, whereas all entities incorporated and operating under Ukrainian law are residents of Ukraine for tax purposes. The place of incorporation is the only criterion, which determines the 'domestic' nature of an entity, and any other criteria (e.g., a place of management) are irrelevant for such consideration. Given this, no dual residency issue arises for legal entities in Ukraine.

[234] The state registration and tax registration of a legal entity are formalized by a record in the state register. The taxpayer is required to register in accordance with the established procedure by filing the required documents to the tax office for tax registration, and tax authorities register the entity in the taxpayers' database. From the moment of tax registration, an entity is considered to be a payer of Corporate Income Tax (CIT).

[235] For corporate income tax purposes, a taxable entity is defined by the Tax Code as a resident legal entity carrying on economic activities both inside and outside the territory of Ukraine, as well as its separate subdivisions. Tax residents are taxed on their worldwide incomes.

[236] The notion of a foreign entity for tax purposes is included in the definition of a non-resident entity. Under the Tax Code, entities established in accordance with foreign law are non-residents for Ukrainian tax purposes. Foreign entities are considered as taxable in Ukraine ('liable to tax') with respect to their Ukrainian-sourced income when they receive such income or have a permanent establishment in Ukraine.

9.3 Main Taxes and Duties

[237] Among approximately twenty-five taxes and duties established by the current Ukrainian legislation, the main taxes and duties are as follows:

- *Corporate Income Tax* (CIT) – CIT is levied on the profit (loss) before tax which is computed as the difference between income and expenses incurred during the reporting period in accordance with UAS or IFRS, subject to certain adjustments, including permitted depreciation deductions. The standard tax rate is 18%. Tax rates of 3% and 0% apply to specific types of insurance premiums, 10% and 18% apply to gambling activities. The standard tax rate applicable to Ukrainian-source income paid to non-resident entities is 15%, and tax rates of 0%, 4%, 6%, 12% apply to various types of such income.
- *Value Added Tax* (VAT) – VAT is paid by the following legal entities, individuals and non-residents' representative offices: (i) any person that is doing business and is willing to be registered as a VAT payer voluntarily; (ii) any person that is registered or shall mandatorily be registered as a VAT payer; (iii) any person that imports goods into Ukraine's customs territory in volumes that are subject to VAT as specified in the Tax Code. VAT registration is required for residents and non-residents if the volume of taxable supplies of goods/services for the previous twelve calendar months exceeded UAH1 000 000 (approx. USD35 260). If the volume of taxable supplies is less than UAH1 000 000 for the previous twelve calendar months, voluntary VAT registration

is available for the qualifying persons mentioned above. The VAT rates are 20%, 7% and 0%, depending on the type of transaction.

- *Personal Income Tax* (PIT) – Standard tax rate of 18% applies to most types of taxable income for both residents and non-residents. The tax rate of 5% applies to dividend income received by resident individuals distributed by Ukrainian resident companies-CIT payers. The rate of 9% applies to dividends distributed by a foreign company (foreign source dividend), by a Ukrainian investment fund or a Ukrainian resident company that pays taxes other than CIT.
- *Military Tax* – temporary military tax at the rate of 1.5% applies to most types of taxable income for both residents and non-residents individuals, including salaries, dividends, capital gains, passive income, etc.
- *Unified Social Tax (UST)* – The unified social tax for employers in 2016 has been set at the level of 22% of the taxable base. The contribution is imposed on employers in respect of employees' salary incomes (previously it varied between 36.76% and 49.7% depending on the level of accident risk applicable to an entity's industry sector). The unified social tax of 22% also applies to the remuneration under civil law contracts. The maximum amount of monthly income to which UST applies is 15 'subsistence minimums' and constitutes UAH75 000 approximately USD2 645.
- *Pension Fund Charges* –Car acquisitions by legal entities and individuals attract a – 3%-5% charge and immovable property acquisitions 1%, based on the asset's value. The use of services on mobile connection attracts a 7.5% charge based on the value of services provided.
- *Excise Duty* – The following goods and products are subject to excise duty: alcohol, alcoholic distillates, alcoholic beverages, beer, tobacco products (including tobacco-containing products for electric heating), certain forms of transportation (cars, car bodies, etc.), petroleum products, liquefied gas and electric power. Excise taxes fall into one of three categories: ad valorem, specific and combined. Ad valorem excise tax is defined as a fixed percentage rate assessed on particular goods, and a specific excise tax is set tax (fixed tax) on a certain product. Combined includes ad valorem and specific excise taxes simultaneously. An importer or producer of excisable goods is required to file a declaration and pay excise tax on a monthly basis. A special electronic administration system is established for administration of excise tax on fuel. All entities engaged in fuel sale must register as excise taxpayers and are required to issue excise invoices and record them electronically in excise invoices registers on each sale operation of fuel.
- *Import Duties* – Import customs duties depend on the classification code under Ukrainian Classification of Goods for Foreign Economic Activity (UKTZED) and the country of origin of the imported goods. The UKTZED classification is based on the 2017 version of the Harmonized System developed by the World Trade Organization. Since Ukraine became a member of the WTO, reduced duty rates apply to goods originating from the WTO countries and countries that granted the 'most favoured nation' status to Ukraine. Ukraine is a party to FTA with the CIS, EFTA (Iceland, Lichtenstein, Norway and Switzerland), Georgia, Macedonia, Montenegro, Canada,

and Israel, and may enjoy zero or reduced customs duty rates, when importing goods, originating from FTA states. Having signed the EU Association agreement, Ukraine commenced a ten year transition period towards a deep and comprehensive free trade zone with the EU. Zero or reduced duty rates apply to goods originating from EU countries. Ukraine is also a signatory to major international customs conventions. Import of assets for the purpose of their contribution by a foreign investor to the charter capital of a Ukrainian entity is exempt from customs duty (unless such goods are intended for further resale or for non-business usage) but is subject to VAT. If such assets are disposed of within three years from the date of import, the entity should pay customs duty.

- *Land Tax* – Land tax is paid by the owners or users of land, individuals and legal entities. The tax rates of 1%, 3%, 5% or 12% depend on the classification, nature and location of the land and on whether the land value has been assessed. The tax rate of up to 3% (except for the agricultural cultivated lands and common-use lands) applies to settled land with a normative monetary value; the tax rate of up to 5% applies to other types of assessable land. The tax rate of up to 12% of the normative monetary value applies to the land plots permanently used by businesses (except for state and communal property). Marginal measure of the land tax rates related to the agricultural cultivated lands is from 0.3% up to 5% of their normative monetary value.
- *Real Estate Tax* – Real estate tax is paid by the owners of residential and non-residential real estate objects, individuals and legal entities. The marginal tax rate on real estate should not exceed 1.5% of the monthly minimum wage as of 1 January of a given year per square metre (currently UAH70.85 per sq. m, approx. USD2.5). Additionally, for taxpayers, owners of residential real estate, where the total area exceeds 300 sq. m (for an apartment) and/or 500 sq. m (for a house), the amount of real estate tax should be increased to UAH25 000 (approx. USD881) annually for each residential property.
- *Stamp Duty* – State duty is charged by court officials, notaries, officials of state bodies when performing certain actions or issuing certain documents (e.g., notarizing contracts, submitting documents to a court, registering information about share issuances). The state duty for the notarization of an agreement for the sale of real estate is 1% of the amount stated in the agreement. In most of the remaining cases the amount of applicable state duty is immaterial. The sale and purchase of shares are exempt from state duty.

9.4 Tax Consolidation: Group Relief of Gains and Losses

[238] There is no concept of group taxation in Ukraine. All group entities assess, pay taxes and file tax returns separately in Ukraine. This, however, does not relate to group taxation in transfer pricing. Anti-BEPS Law defines the international group of companies as two or more legal persons or entities without the status of a legal person that are tax residents of different countries and are related to each other by ownership of control criteria.

A three-level model for filing reports on controlled transactions carried out by Ukrainian residents belonging to international groups of companies has been introduced:

(1) A local report on controlled transactions.
(2) A request for the master file can be received by a company if the total consolidated income of an international group of companies amounts to EUR50m or more.
(3) A country-by-country report shall be filed by a company if the total consolidated income of an international group of companies amounts to EUR750m.

9.5 Tax Considerations Arising on M&A Transactions

[239] The principal parties in M&A transactions should consider the following income tax implications:

On a sale of shares:

(i) From the vendor's perspective:
- *Individual vendor*: The seller should consider the PIT implications for capital gains from disposal of shares/corporate rights. Income from sale of investment assets is subject to PIT at standard 18% rates as well as military tax at the rate of 1.5%.
- *Corporate vendor*: The Ukrainian seller should consider the CIT implications for capital gains on disposal of shares/corporate rights. Capital gains are subject to CIT at a standard 18% rate. The non-resident seller of the shares or equity interest in the Ukrainian company should consider the withholding tax implications for capital gains. The withholding tax of 15% applies, subject to double tax treaty provisions.
- *Corporate non-resident vendor*: Capital gains derived by a non-resident seller from, the direct or indirect, sale of the shares or equity interest of a Ukrainian real estate rich company is subject to 15% withholding tax, subject to applicable double tax treaty provisions. A Ukrainian company is qualified as 'real estate rich' if at any time during the 365 days preceding the alienation, these shares or equity interests in a Ukrainian company derived at least 50% of their value from immovable property situated in Ukraine and owned by such a Ukrainian company or leased by it under a long-term lease agreement. A non-resident purchaser is a responsible tax agent and is liable to determine the capital gain and withhold 15% tax from such capital gain. A non-resident purchaser shall register with Ukrainian tax authority before processing payment for the purchase of shares/equity interest, file a relevant tax return and pay tax to the state budget.

(ii) From the purchaser's perspective:
- *Individual purchaser*: The purchaser should consider that he/she will be able to deduct the acquisition costs for PIT purposes only when the acquired shares/corporate rights are subsequently disposed of. Income from sale of investment assets (investment income) is subject to PIT at a standard 18% rate as well as military tax at the rate of 1.5%.
- *Corporate purchaser*: The Ukrainian purchaser should consider that it will be able to deduct the purchase price for CIT purposes only when the acquired shares/corporate rights are subsequently disposed of. Capital gains are subject to CIT at a standard 18% rate.

On a sale of assets:

(i) From the vendor's perspective:
- *Individual vendor*: Gross revenue from the sale of real estate and movable assets is subject to PIT. Cost of such assets cannot be deducted. For Ukrainian residents, the rates of 0% and 5% apply for the sale of real estate and 5% – for the sale of movable assets. For foreign individuals, the standard rates of 18% are applicable to the disposal of all above-mentioned types of property as well as military tax at the rate of 1.5%.
- *Corporate vendor*: The Ukrainian seller should consider the CIT implications for realized gains on disposition of assets. Such gains are subject to CIT at a standard 18% rate. The non-resident seller of real estate situated on the territory of Ukraine should consider the withholding tax implications for capital gains from such disposal. The withholding tax of 15% applies, subject to double tax treaty provisions.

(ii) From the purchaser's perspective:
- *Individual purchaser*: Both for real estate and movable assets, cost of property cannot be deducted for PIT purposes by the individual.
- Corporate purchaser: The Ukrainian purchaser is permitted tax deduction/depreciation/amortization of the costs of purchased assets.

[240] Where the purchaser is a Ukrainian company, indirect expenses incurred in connection with the acquisition (such as legal or accounting fees) will generally be deductible.

9.6 Controlled Foreign Companies (CFC) Rules

[241] Anti-BEPS Law introduced CFC rules, which become effective starting from 1 January 2021 (with potential postponement). Both individuals and legal entities resident in Ukraine that own or control a CFC shall submit a CFC report together with an applicable tax return for the relevant calendar year.

A foreign legal person or entity shall be deemed a controlled foreign company in Ukraine if an individual or a legal entity resident in Ukraine (directly or indirectly):

(i) possesses more than 50% shareholding in the foreign legal person (entity); or
(ii) possesses more than 10% (25% until 2022 inclusive) shareholding in the foreign legal person (entity), provided several individuals and/or legal persons resident in Ukraine jointly hold at least a 50% shareholding in that foreign legal person; or
(iii) independently or jointly with other related parties resident in Ukraine exercises actual control over the foreign legal person (entity), i.e. is capable of exerting significant or decisive influence on the decisions passed by such a foreign legal person (entity) with respect to concluding transactions, assets and profits management, termination of activities, regardless of how such influence is registered from a legal point of view.

Profits earned by a CFC shall be included in aggregate taxable income of a Ukrainian resident and be subject to taxation in Ukraine:

(1) 18% personal income tax plus 1.5% military tax, if a CFC is controlled by an individual resident in Ukraine;
(2) 18% corporate tax, if a CFC is controlled by a legal entity resident in Ukraine.

If a CFC has distributed its profits to its controlling person resident in Ukraine in the form of dividends, such CFC's profits shall not be included in aggregate taxable income.

The CFC's profits should be exempt from taxation in Ukraine if at least one of the following conditions is fulfilled:

(a) Ukraine has a double tax treaty with CFC's country *and* either one of the following criteria is satisfied:
   - CFC pays corporate tax at an effective rate of 13% or higher; or
   - the share of CFC's passive income (dividends, interest, royalties, income from securities trading, etc.) does not exceed 50%;
(b) the total income of all CFCs controlled by a Ukrainian resident does not exceed EUR2m a year;
(c) CFC is a publicly-traded company listed on a recognized stock exchange;
(d) CFC is a charitable organization.

9.7 Structuring the Investment: Withholding Taxes

[242] Ukrainian-source income payable to a non-resident (except for a permanent establishment of a foreign entity) by a Ukrainian resident or a permanent establishment of a foreign entity is subject to withholding tax.

[243] Ukrainian-source income includes the following main types of income: interest, dividends, royalties, income payable for freight or engineering services, leasing (rental) income, income from the disposal of immovable property located in Ukraine, gains from trade in securities or other corporate rights, income from unincorporated joint ventures in Ukraine, income from operations under long-term agreements in Ukraine, agent fees, premiums for (re)insurance of risks in Ukraine or insurance of residents from risks abroad.

[244] Payable proceeds or other compensation for goods and services (supplied by a non-resident or its permanent establishment to a Ukrainian resident) do not qualify as Ukrainian-source income and, therefore, are not subject to withholding tax, unless such transactions are executed between the related parties and payable proceeds exceed the arm's-length price for such goods or services. In this case, the excess amount should be treated as Ukrainian source dividends subject to withholding tax.

[245] The standard withholding tax rate is 15%. A special tax rate is established for freight income (6%). Potentially, the withholding tax rate can be reduced based on a relevant double tax treaty. However, because Ukraine ratified Multilateral Convention to implement tax treat- related measures to prevent BEPS (MLI) and adopted Anti-BEPS Law the application of tax benefits (tax relief or a reduced tax rate) provided for by an applicable double tax treaty can be limited or denied in Ukraine.

[246] A Ukrainian resident's payment to a non-resident for the production or distribution of advertising materials is subject to a 20% tax charge payable by the Ukrainian resident from out of its own funds (i.e., not withheld). Insurance premiums and compensatory payments made under insurance and re-insurance agreements are taxed at special rates (0%, 4% or 12%) from out of the Ukrainian taxpayer's own funds. Ukrainian taxpayers cannot enjoy treaty protection in respect of these types of income.

[247] A Ukrainian taxpayer is obliged to withhold tax from the Ukrainian-source income or pay tax from its own funds to the state on the date of income remittance.

[248] In particular, dividends, interest, royalties and some other payments to non-residents are taxed in the following way:

- *Dividends paid to foreign corporate/group shareholders*: Dividend payments to non-resident legal entities are subject to withholding tax at a standard rate of 15% that can be reduced based on a relevant double tax treaty. No tax deduction can be allowed in respect of such payments. A company distributing dividends to its shareholders must pay an advance CIT (ACT) calculated at a standard CIT rate over the gross amount of the dividends intended for the payment without reducing the amount of such payment by the amount of such ACT (i.e., ACT is not withheld). The company should pay the ACT to the state budget before or concurrently with the payment of dividends to the shareholders. The company can reduce its CIT liability by the amount of ACT paid in the reporting period (year) when the dividend payment occurred. Any unutilized ACT balance can be carried forward to future periods. ACT is not refunded by the state. ACT does not apply to payments of dividends distributed in the form of shares provided that such share issuance does not dilute existing shareholders' equity in the company's charter capital. ACT also does not apply to investment funds and in certain other cases.

- *Dividends paid to foreign individual shareholders*: Dividend payments to foreign individuals are subject to PIT at a rate of 5% that can be reduced based on a relevant double tax treaty. No tax deduction can be allowed in respect of such payments. No ACT should be paid in respect of such payments.
- *Dividends received from foreign subsidiaries/affiliates:* Such dividends are included in taxable income for CIT purposes.
- *Interest paid to foreign corporate/group shareholders or affiliates*: Interest payments to non-residents are subject to withholding tax at a standard rate of 15% that can be reduced based on a relevant double tax treaty. Deduction of such payments is subject to quasi thin capitalization rule that is explained in more detail below.
- *Interest received from foreign corporate/group shareholders or affiliates:* Such interest is included in taxable income for CIT purposes.
- *Intellectual property (IP) royalties paid to foreign corporate/group shareholders or affiliates:* Royalty payments to non-residents are subject to withholding tax at a standard rate of 15% that can be reduced based on a relevant double tax treaty. No tax deduction can be allowed in respect of the royalties accrued in favour of non-residents in an amount exceeding 4% of the prior year's sales revenue (this limitation does not apply to the expenses incurred in respect of the non-residents' permanent establishments). The tax deduction of these expenses is entirely prohibited if they are incurred in favour of the residents of low tax jurisdictions, non-residents that are not beneficial owners, as well as in certain other instances.
- *IP royalties received from foreign corporate/group shareholders or affiliates*: Such royalties are included in taxable income for CIT purposes.
- *Consultancy fees paid to foreign corporate/group shareholders or affiliates*: Consultancy fees paid to non-residents are not subject to withholding tax.
- *Payments to non-residents in respect of the purchase or lease of immovable property*: 15% withholding tax applies to non-resident's income on the sale of real estate and lease fees.

[249] Ukraine has a wide network of double tax treaties in force on the avoidance of double taxation. Treaties allow for the reduction of the withholding tax rate for dividends, interest or royalties to 0%, 2%, 3%, 5%, 7%, 7.5%, 10%, 12%.

[250] A Ukrainian taxpayer may obtain relief from the obligation to withhold tax or reduce the applicable withholding tax rate provided that all of the following requirements are met:

(a) a foreign recipient of income is a resident of the state with which Ukraine has an effective treaty on the avoidance of double taxation;
(b) a non-resident has provided a residence certificate issued by the authorities of the counterpart treaty country; and
(c) a non-resident income recipient satisfies qualification criteria envisaged in the relevant double tax treaty.

[251] A Ukrainian bank or a financial institution paying interest to a non-resident bank can enjoy treaty protection if such payer provides an extract from the international catalogue 'International Bank Identifier Code' confirming that the recipient (the non-resident bank) is a resident of a counterpart treaty country. In this case, a Ukrainian payer is not required to obtain a residence certificate from the recipient.

[252] One of the most favourable treaties for foreign investors is the Ukraine-Cyprus double tax treaty, which provides for 5%, 5% and 5/0% withholding tax rates on the payment of dividends, interest and royalties, respectively. Such rates are low and competitive with the rates under Ukraine's other double tax treaties. The Ukrainian withholding tax on interest or royalty payments can potentially be set off against the Cypriot tax attributable to the respective types of such income. The overall tax regime of Cyprus is attractive for investing in Ukraine and competitive as compared with other jurisdictions. At the same time, Ukraine and Cyprus have already implemented the MLI and, therefore, starting from 1 January 2021, the Principal Purpose Test needs to be satisfied to obtain tax benefits under the Ukraine/Cyprus Tax Treaty.

[253] Ukraine had favourable treaties with the Netherlands, Switzerland, Austria, Sweden, and the UK. The double tax treaties between Ukraine and these countries provide for attractive withholding tax rates on Ukrainian-source income: 0% and 5% – for dividend distribution, 0% and 2% – for interest payments, and 0% – for payments of certain types of royalties. The Principal Purpose Test and other provisions of the MLI are already applicable with respect to the double tax treaties with the UK and Sweden and prevent the use of the tax treaties to achieve a double non-taxation effect or the creation of indirect benefits for residents of third countries.

9.8 Thin Capitalization

[254] The following rules apply to legal persons starting from 1 January 2021. The thin capitalization ratio is set at 3.5:1. Should the total aggregate amount of the borrowings received from all non-residents exceed the equity of the borrower by 3.5 or more times, the borrower is allowed to recognize as expenses interest payments in an amount not exceeding 30% of the CIT base increased with the amount of financial expenses under accounting rules and tax depreciation. Interest expenses above the limit could be carried forward and be deducted in computing CIT. Interest includes liabilities on loans, deposits, REPO transactions, financial lease agreements and other borrowings. If the debt to equity ratio is less than 3.5:1, interest is deductible in full.

Interest that has been capitalized as part of the value of non-current assets shall be included with interest expenses proportionately to the depreciation of such assets for the respective reporting period. If the amount of interest expenses within a controlled transaction exceeds the amount determined in accordance with the arm's-length principle, then thin capitalization rules will apply only to the amount of interest that corresponds with the arm's-length principle.

The thin capitalization rules will no longer apply to financial institutions and companies engaged exclusively in leasing activities.

9.9 Transfer Pricing

[255] In 2013, transfer pricing rules were introduced in Ukraine. Such rules applied for calculation of CIT and VAT charges, but, since July 2015, transfer pricing rules apply to CIT only and require that qualifying transactions (so-called controlled transactions) be taxed on the basis of the principle of the arm's-length value of the transaction.

Anti-BEPS Law introduced certain amendments to transfer pricing rules, which, in particular, apply to international groups of companies.

[256] A three-level model for filing reports on controlled operations carried out by Ukrainian residents belonging to international groups of companies has been introduced:

- A local report on controlled transactions;
- A request for the master file can be received by a company if the total consolidated income of an international group of companies amounts to EUR50 million or more;
- A country-by-country report shall be filed by a company if the total consolidated income of an international group of companies amounts to EUR750 million.

Such reporting will be subject to automatic exchange of tax and financial information after the common reporting system will be implemented in Ukraine.

[257] A transaction with a counterparty is considered to be controlled if two conditions are met: (i) the volume of transaction(s) with one counterparty exceeds UAH10 000 000 (approx. USD352 600), net of VAT, and (ii) the taxpayers' annual income exceeds UAH150 000 000 (approx. USD5 289 000), net of VAT, and (iii) such transactions falls within one of the following types:

(1) Transactions with foreign entities, related parties.
(2) Foreign trade transactions through agents (commissioners) foreign companies.
(3) Transactions with non-residents that are registered in or are residents of jurisdictions listed in the Resolution of the Cabinet of Ministers of Ukraine No. 1045 dated 27 December 2017.
(4) Transactions with non-residents that do not pay CIT, including on revenues received outside of the state of registration of such non-residents, and/or that are not tax residents of the country where they are registered as legal entities. The list of organizational and legal forms of such non-residents in terms of states (territories) is established by the Resolution of the Cabinet of Ministers of Ukraine No. 480 dated 4 July 2017. If such non-residents pay CIT in the reporting year, the transactions with such

non-residents are not considered as controlled if other criteria for the recognition of controlled transactions are not met.

(5) Transactions with related non-residents if between them several unrelated persons are interposed that do not perform significant functions / assume significant risks;

(6) Transactions between non-residents and their permanent establishments registered in Ukraine.

[258] Generally, Ukrainian legislation provides for five transfer pricing methods:

(1) Comparable uncontrolled price method.
(2) Resale price method.
(3) Cost plus method.
(4) Transactional net margin method.
(5) Profit split method.

[259] Taxpayers that conducted controlled transactions during the reporting year should file a report electronically on such transactions by the first of October of the year following the reporting year. For failure to file such report, a taxpayer should pay a financial penalty.

[260] However, paying penalties does not exempt the taxpayer from its obligation to file a report on a controlled transaction or prepare transfer pricing documentation.

10. ACCOUNTING TREATMENT

[261] Ukrainian legislation requires that listed companies, banks and insurers prepare their financial statements according to the IFRS while other companies have been given the discretion to adopt them or not. In practice, many Ukrainian companies with foreign investment (in particular, those seeking to raise financing on international capital markets) adopt IFRS and have their accounts audited by international accounting firms in accordance with International Standards on Auditing. The remaining Ukrainian companies often prepare their financial reports for tax purposes rather than as a means of establishing their financial state.

[262] The Ukrainian domestic accounting standards are approved by the Ministry of Finance of Ukraine. They determine, in particular, the format and content of group accounts for Ukrainian parent companies.

[263] According to the Ukrainian GAAP, mergers and acquisitions have the following accounting treatment.

[264] If the company is being liquidated as a result of acquisition of its net assets by another company, then the buyer should report the assets and liabilities of the target company, as well as any goodwill arising as a result of such acquisition, in its balance sheet starting from the date of acquisition.

[265] In case of acquisition of a controlling interest in another company, the buyer should report the acquired shares/participation interest as a financial investment starting from the date of acquisition.

[266] If the buyer acquires the target company step-by-step (e.g., by a serial acquisition of shares), then the purchaser evaluates financial investments in the target company at their fair value at the date of acquisition and includes the amount of change in such value in income or expenses.

[267] The date of acquisition is defined as a date when the acquiring company gets control over the net assets and activities of the target company.

[268] Goodwill is not amortized and is subject to impairment review at the end of each year. If goodwill does not meet the criteria to be recognized as an asset, it should be written down, and its balance sheet carrying value should be included in expenses. Negative goodwill is not recognized as a balance sheet item and is credited to the profit and loss account.

[269] If the costs of any reorganization and/or integration of the acquired business are incurred in the current period but relate to future periods, they are recognized as an asset called 'Expenses of Future Periods' and written down in such future periods to which they relate.

[270] Intangible assets are recognized if it is probable that the future economic benefits that are attributable to the asset will flow to the entity, and the cost of the asset can be measured reliably. Intangible assets are amortized over their useful lives and should also be assessed for impairment.

[271] From the vendor's perspective, income and expenses from the sale of financial investments should be reported as 'Other Income' and 'Other Expenses', respectively. They affect the profit/loss from ordinary activities.

11. EMPLOYMENT CONSIDERATIONS

11.1 Legislative Framework

[272] Labour relations in Ukraine are still governed by the labour code adopted during the Soviet era – the Labour Code of Ukraine, dated 10 December 1971 (Labour Code). Provisions of the Labour Code extend to all employees and employers in Ukraine irrespective of the form of ownership or type of business (where the employer is a legal entity). Although being the cornerstone of the employment legislation, the Labour Code is not the sole statute regulating labour relations, and there are also numerous acts governing vacations, collective bargaining agreements, foreign labour, trade unions, etc.

[273] The Labour Code is regarded as being heavily pro-employee and prohibits an employer from reducing an employee's rights through a labour agreement. Despite the numerous changes introduced to the Labour Code since Ukraine's independence it is nonetheless outdated and does not adequately take into consideration current economic conditions. Many foreign investors thus find that the Labour Code decreases their flexibility in managing their labour relations in Ukraine.

[274] The Ukrainian Parliament has undertaken several attempts to modernize employment relationships and adopt a new labour code. At this writing, it remains unclear when a new law would be enacted reflecting the contemporary labour market and creating an environment where businesses can thrive alongside adequate labour safeguards.

11.2 Employment Agreements

[275] An employment agreement may be of: (a) unlimited duration (i.e., concluded for an indefinite term); (b) fixed duration as agreed by the parties; or (c) such duration as may be needed to perform a specific job. Ukrainian labour law generally encourages permanent employment, i.e., employment agreements for an indefinite term. An employment agreement of fixed duration may only be concluded in cases where permanent employment is not possible due to the specific nature of the job, specific conditions of its performance or in the interests of an employee, and in certain other cases stipulated by law.

[276] An employment agreement is generally concluded in writing, although it is not mandatory in all cases. However, a written agreement is required by law: (1) in the event of organized public recruitment of labour; (2) when concluding an agreement for work in areas with special geographical and geological conditions and other conditions presenting a higher health risk; (3) when concluding an employment contract; (4) in those cases when an employee insists on a written agreement; (5) when concluding an employment agreement with a minor; (6) when concluding an employment agreement with an employer who is an individual; or (7) when concluding an employment agreement establishing a remote work (work at home) regime for employees.

[277] An employment contract is a special form of employment agreement and may be used only where expressly permitted by law (e.g., with company managing directors/CEOs, employees of a commodity exchange, associate attorneys and employees of educational institutions). Generally, an employment contract gives the parties more discretion in determining their respective rights and obligations, including those with respect to working conditions, termination, compensation, and benefits. In other words, the parties to an employment contract may include provisions that differ from those prescribed by the Labour Code, such as additional grounds for liability and termination of employment. An employment contract usually provides various benefits to an employee as compensation for the contract's limited duration. Such benefits may include, for example, a longer annual vacation, higher additional payments to the salary and/or more flexible working hours

than the respective standards provided by the Labour Code. Neither an employment contract nor an employment agreement may diminish the employment guarantees provided by the Labour Code, other labour laws and regulations, and any applicable collective bargaining agreement. Provisions of the employment agreement or contract which worsen an employee's position as compared to the Labour Code are considered null and void.

11.3 Labour Costs and Working Conditions

11.3.1 Salary

[278] The amount of salary payable to the employee is agreed between the employer and employee but may not be lower than the minimum monthly salary established by the applicable annual budget law. Currently, the minimum monthly salary for 2021 is set at UAH6 000 (ca. USD215).

[279] The salary should be paid in two semi-monthly instalments: portion of the salary for the first part of the month – the advance payment and portion of the salary for the second part of the month – the principal payment, with an interval between the two instalments not exceeding sixteen calendar days, and no later than on the seventh day following the period for which the salary is paid. The amount of the first instalment should not be less than a part of the employee's base salary which is proportional to the amount of time worked by the employee that month.

11.3.2 Working Time; Days Off; Holidays

[280] As a general rule, duration of working hours may not exceed forty hours per week. For certain categories of employees (e.g., minors, employees working in hazardous labour conditions) Ukrainian labour laws establish a reduced workweek. Any hours worked by the employee in excess of the regular working hours are considered overtime hours and may be required only in exceptional circumstances. As a rule, overtime is not allowed. Involvement of employees in overtime work is subject to consent with the trade union (if one has been created with the employer). Overtime work is prohibited for pregnant women, women with minor children under 3 years old; minors under 18 years old; employees studying part-time at general secondary and vocational schools on the day of study. Overtime work for women with minor children between 3 and 14 years old or with a disabled child is permitted only with the employee's consent. Overtime work for a disabled person is permitted only with the employee's consent and provided that the work does not contradict any medical recommendations applicable to the employee. Overtime work may not exceed 4 hours within 2 consecutive days and 120 hours in total per annum.

In some cases, it is possible to establish an unlimited workday schedule, whereby an employee may be required to or must at his/her own initiative stay at work beyond regular working hours if so dictated by his/her duties, and such extra working hours are not considered overtime. However, employees working unlimited workday schedule are entitled to additional paid vacation of up to seven calendar days.

[281] Employees are entitled to two days off if working on a five-day workweek, such days generally being Saturday and Sunday, and to one day off, generally being Sunday, if working on a six-day workweek.

[282] The Labour Code establishes the following official holidays in Ukraine: New Year's Day (1 January); Orthodox Christmas (7 January); International Women's Day (8 March); Days of International Solidarity of Employees (1 May); Victory Day (9 May); Constitution Day (28 June); Ukraine's Independence Day (24 August), Defender of the Fatherland Day (14 October), Christmas (24 December) and on Easter and Trinity Sundays. Employees may only be required to work on these days in exceptional circumstances.

[283] Overtime work must be compensated by the employer at double the regular hourly rate, and in the case of work on a day off or a holiday – at double the regular hourly rate or by providing an additional day off, as agreed by the parties.

11.3.3 Vacation

[284] All employees working in Ukraine must be provided with an annual vacation of at least twenty-four calendar days for each working year. Such vacation is provided with guaranteed retention of employment (rank/position) and salary. Certain categories of employees are entitled to longer basic vacations and/or additional annual vacations, the latter being granted to employees such as those, for example, working in hazardous and difficult labour conditions.

11.3.4 Sick Leave

[285] The first five days of sick leave, which should be evidenced by a medical certificate, are paid by the employer, and the remaining sick period is compensated from the Social Security Fund on Temporary Loss of Working Capacity. Depending on the length of employment, a sick period is paid to an employee in full or in part.

11.4 Treatment of Foreign Employees

[286] Ukrainian law generally allows hiring foreign nationals and offers them equal benefits and protections available to Ukrainian employees under applicable Ukrainian laws. There are, however, some restrictions on the type of positions that a foreign national can hold. For example, foreign nationals may not be appointed to the positions which require Ukrainian citizenship (e.g., state service jobs) or positions that require access to state secrets.

[287] As a general rule, in order to hire a foreigner, an employer must obtain a work permit for that foreigner. The procedure for obtaining a work permit is envisaged by the Law of Ukraine On Employment dated 5 July 2012.

[288] To obtain a work permit, an employer should submit a work permit application together with supporting documents to a respective employment centre. The employment centre has to decide on a work permit application accompanied by the supporting documents within seven business days of its receipt. Within ten business days starting from the date of obtaining (receipt) of the decision on issuance of the work permit, the employer should pay the state fee for work permit varying from two to six times the minimum subsistence level. In 2021, if the work permit is issued for the period of up to six months – UAH4 540 (USD162), or between six months and 1 year – UAH9 080 (USD324), or more than one year but less than three years – UAH13 620 (USD486). Failure by the employer to make the payment within the established time frame will result in cancellation of the rendered decision. The employment centre issues a work permit to the employer within three business days of the date of receiving the fee from the employer. Thus, the overall process for obtaining a work permit may take around one month.

[289] A work permit is generally issued for a term of up to one year and can be extended for the same term. Work permits for intra-group transferees and persons rendering services in Ukraine without establishing commercial presence in Ukraine are issued for a term of up to three years and can be extended for two years.

[290] Employment of a foreign national without a valid work permit, or on terms other than those provided in a work permit, may result in a fine on the employer in the amount of twenty statutory minimum monthly salaries (currently, UAH120 000 (ca. USD4 285)) or ten statutory minimum monthly salaries (currently, UAH60 000 (ca. USD2 140)), respectively.

[291] Ukrainian law does not prohibit foreign nationals from holding top management positions in Ukrainian companies. Foreign directors working in Ukraine, similarly to Ukrainian nationals, are exposed to civil, administrative, disciplinary and criminal liability. Although it is theoretically possible to insure such liability, in practice obtaining directors & officers liability insurance (D&O) is rather uncommon in Ukraine and there are only a few insurance companies which offer such D&O coverage.

11.5 Employee Representation

[292] Employees may participate in management of a company through trade unions. Under the Law of Ukraine 'On Trade Unions, Its Rights and Guarantees' dated 15 September 1999, Ukrainian employees are free to establish and participate in trade unions in any company. Foreign employees may only become members of existing trade unions unless otherwise provided by the trade union's statutory provisions.

[293] A trade union functions within a company through its elected body or a representative, and its powers are rather broad. Trade unions represent interests of employees in collective negotiations, conclusion of a collective bargaining agreement and control over its implementation. Together with an employer, a trade union decides on issues of remuneration, bonuses, working hours and rest periods, guarantees, compensations, privileges, and other labour issues of trade union members. A trade union may initiate dismissal of a company's director for breaching labour legislation, deviating from concluding or amending a collective bargaining agreement, non-performing under the collective bargaining agreement and breaching other legislation concerning collective bargaining agreements. Trade unions also monitor an employer's compliance with labour laws, including labour protection laws, and proper implementation of established remuneration terms. For this purpose, a trade union is entitled to request from company's official servicers all documents relating to compliance with labour legislation and observation of the collective bargaining agreement and demand rectification of any identified violations.

[294] Employers are obliged to support creation of proper conditions for the trade union activities (e.g., to provide equipped rooms for meetings) and to allocate funds of at least 0.3% of the company's salary fund for cultural, recreational and health-improving activities. In addition, employers must, within one week of a request, provide trade unions with information on labour conditions, terms of employees' remuneration, social and economic development of the company, and implementation of the collective bargaining agreement.

11.6 Termination of Employment

[295] As a general rule, an employee may terminate his/her employment at any time by giving two weeks' notice to the employer. Such notice period may be shortened in the event that there are valid reasons requiring the employee to be dismissed on a shorter notice, and the employer will be required to dismiss the employee within the requested term. An employee working under a fixed-term employment agreement may at his/her initiative terminate it prior to its expiry only in cases provided by law.

[296] Employment may also be terminated at any time and for any reason by mutual consent of an employer and an employee. This option for termination of employment allows the parties to negotiate the terms and conditions of termination and post-termination commitments of the parties, if applicable.

[297] An employer may unilaterally initiate termination of employment in limited cases and only upon specific grounds set forth in the Labour Code. These grounds include liquidation, reorganization, bankruptcy, or restructuring of the company, including staff reductions; unsuitable employment qualifications or physical condition of the employee; systematic and inexcusable failure of the employee to observe the requirements of the employment agreement or the employer's internal rules and regulations; unjustified absence from work (including absence for more than three hours during the working day); drunkenness on the job or public intoxication caused by drugs or other intoxicants; and other cases provided by Articles 40 and

41 of the Labour Code. In some of these cases: (i) the employee may be dismissed only with the prior consent of the relevant trade union (if there is one); and (ii) the employee may be entitled to statutory severance pay in the amount of up to three average monthly salaries.

[298] In addition, the employee may not be dismissed upon the initiative of the employer while on vacation or while temporarily disabled, except on the ground of failure to report to work for more than four consecutive months as a result of a temporary disability or in the event of liquidation of the company.

[299] Certain categories of employees, such as pregnant women, women with children under the age of three, single mothers with children under the age of 14 or with disabled children, enjoy special protection against dismissal on any legal ground at the employer's initiative, except in the event of liquidation of the company. In this latter exception, the affected employees may be dismissed provided that their employer secures their further employment with another company.

[300] The Labour Code establishes other grounds for termination of employment which include expiration of the term of the employment agreement; entry of the employee into military or alternative non-military service; at the initiative of the relevant trade union (if any); transfer of an employee, with his/her consent, to another company or to an elected position; employee's refusal to move to another location or continue work because of a change in principal labour conditions; a court decision sentencing the employee to imprisonment or imposing other punishment that makes further employment impossible; or reasons specified in a labour contract.

11.7 Transfer of Business

11.7.1 Continuity on Business Transfers

[301] Generally, transfer of business by way of a sale of shares in a JSC or participatory interests in an LLC do not affect employees of the business from the legal point of view. Employment agreements with the company's employees remain in place and the employees of such company are considered to be automatically transferred to a purchaser of a business by operation of law. The new business owner will be restricted in his ability to unilaterally dismiss employees for reasons other than a workforce reduction. In addition, the Labour Code provides for an extension of the collective bargaining agreement to the new business owner following the business transfer.

[302] In asset transactions, depending on the deal structure, the purchaser of the business is generally able to pre-select those employees of the target company he wishes to retain, and such employees must consent to transfer (often by agreeing to a termination of their employment with the seller and accepting new employment with the purchaser).

[303] It is common for Ukrainian companies to have trade unions which serve as employee representatives and have the right to receive information and to be consulted on issues and decisions which can affect employees. Such information and consultation obligations of the employer often exist before the trade unions and employees in stock and asset transactions which contemplate, among other things, transfer of some, but not all, employees, redundancies or changes in the terms of employment.

11.7.2 Retention of Key Employees

[304] An important consideration for the purchaser is the retention of key employees during and after the acquisition process. 'Stay' bonuses are the most popular means of retaining executives and other key employees of the business. Such bonuses are awarded as a percentage of salary or a lump sum amount, can be paid immediately or over time, and can be structured in tiers. Other incentives may include performance-based bonuses and 'golden parachutes'. These incentives can be implemented by either the purchaser or the seller and quite often by both.

11.7.3 Non-compete Covenants

[305] As part of an M&A deal, the parties often enter into various restrictive covenants, such as an obligation of the seller not to compete with the target for a period of time after closing, so as to ensure that the target's trade secrets, business connections and practices are preserved and the purchaser is entitled to a maximum return on its investment. In the EU such restrictions are characterized as ancillary restrictions and are automatically permitted as part of the merger clearance to the extent they are directly related, necessary and proportionate to the implementation of the concentration. The Ukrainian competition legislation has a different approach and requires the parties to obtain prior AMC approval for such non-compete obligations, known as concerted actions that would specifically permit restriction of competition between the parties. Such approval would be in addition to the AMC approval for the M&A transaction. Agreements providing for a non-compete obligation must envisage that such obligation will only take effect upon obtaining concerted actions approval from the AMC.

[306] In the employment context, non-compete provisions included in employment contracts are generally enforceable only to the extent they limit an employee's right to have a second job while employed by a company. Post-termination non-compete provisions are generally unenforceable, as they are viewed as restricting the employee's right to work and entrepreneurial activity granted by the Constitution of Ukraine and other applicable legislation (*see* 'Merger Controls: Antitrust/Competition Issues' for information on anticompetitive restraints).

www.ingramcontent.com/pod-product-compliance
Ingram Content Group UK Ltd.
Pitfield, Milton Keynes, MK11 3LW, UK
UKHW020151290926
15471UKWH00004B/806

9 789403 540115